CW00649898

"As someone who was blown away by Farah Harris' expertise, humility, authenticity, and her ability to simplify complex concepts into an accessible format during her appearance on the Negotiate Anything Podcast, I was eager to read her book *The Color of Emotional Intelligence*.

"I must say that this book exceeded my already high expectations. It speaks to a wide range of individuals, including those who didn't realize they were tired of showing up for everyone else but themselves, those who have been historically and systemically marginalized, traumatized, and aggressed, and those who work in diversity, equity, and inclusion. It also provides valuable insights for leaders who want to better support their employees, especially those from underrepresented groups, and allies who want to make the world a better place.

"Farah's book is a refreshing and much-needed addition to the literature on emotional intelligence, providing practical and insightful advice on how to elevate our emotional intelligence as part of our personal development. It highlights the role that emotional intelligence plays in how we live, see ourselves, and interact with others, and it emphasizes the importance of courage, empathy, and effective communication beyond just interpersonal skills.

"I highly recommend *The Color of Emotional Intelligence* to anyone seeking to improve their emotional intelligence and overall well-being. Farah's expertise, humility, and authenticity shine through every page, making this book a valuable and enjoyable read for anyone looking to grow in awareness and cultivate emotional intelligence in their personal and professional lives."

— Kwame Christian Esq., M.A.,
Founder and CEO of the American Negotiation Institute

"A brilliant balance between theory and practice, *The Color of Emotional Intelligence: Elevating Our Self and Social Awareness to Address Inequities* should be in everyone's 'doing life' toolkit. Thirst-quenching and soul-edifying, while also being practical and action-oriented, this is the comprehensive resource you never knew you always needed. Renowned expert Farah Harris has outdone herself. As she so rightly affirms, there is nothing soft about the skills we need to regulate ourselves, to navigate our relationships and our world. . . and to address inequities. Emotional intelligence is a 'strengths skill.' This book explains why it matters."

— Theresa M. Robinson, DEI, Anti-Racism,
Well-Being Educator and ATD-certified Master Trainer

"Farah's work offers a necessary perspective shift in emotional intelligence beyond the dominant White male perspective. Managing our emotions is a critical part of allyship. These proven strategies help people take real action towards positive change."

— Julie Kratz,
Author of *Allyship in Action* and DEI speaker

"*The Color of Emotional Intelligence* was a life-changing read for me that should be required reading in every leadership development program. Farah gave one of the best explanations of EI, racism, and allyship/stewardship that I've seen, and illuminated how EI provides a tool for justice and healing. She transformed EI from a business buzzword into a tool that can be used, in her words, to 'create a world where we all feel safe to be our best selves because we decided to show up as our best selves for others.'"

— Teri Schmidt, Director & Leadership Coach,
Stronger to Serve Coaching & Teambuilding

"True growth requires us to ask new questions, consider new perspectives, and try new things. With relatable examples and a refreshing sense of humor, Farah guides us toward a greater degree of emotional intelligence and, on the way, challenges everything we think we know about this critical relationship skill."

— Tara Jaye Frank,
Author of *The Waymakers: Clearing the Path to Workplace Equity with Competence and Confidence*, and C-Suite workplace consultant

"How can we lead inclusively using frameworks defined almost exclusively from the white male perspective? Long overdue, Farah Harris explores the critically important concept of emotional intelligence through an equity lens. It's an important read for emerging leaders and seasoned executives alike."

— Dana Brownlee, Workplace Anti-Racism Thought Leader

"Profound. Thought provoking. Necessary. Farah Harris expertly illustrates how the power of emotional intelligence can protect us and how it can further connect us, if we choose. Focusing on the intersection of EQ and equity, Harris provides a unique and critical expansion on this practice that has been long dominated by White male researchers' perspectives. She takes you on a transformational journey through worlds you may not see and helps you see your world differently. This is the EQ book I didn't realize I was waiting for, and the one our current world needs!"

— Sarah Noll Wilson,
Executive Coach and Author of *Don't Feed the Elephants: Overcoming the Art of Avoidance for Powerful Partnerships*

"As a coach that works with people leaders, I tell my clients that emotional intelligence is among the top skills required for next-level leadership. *The Color of Emotional Intelligence* does just that.

"Farah provides leaders with a blueprint for not just understanding themselves but also explains the experiences of those that face micro- (and macro-) aggressions daily. She reveals the challenges minoritized employees face and equips leaders with the tools needed to increase their EQ. This is a must-read for 21st-century inclusive leadership."

— Sacha Thompson, ACC,
Inclusive Culture Curator and Founder, The Equity Equation

"Farah has crafted a masterpiece on emotional intelligence, the layers of emotional intelligence, and its important nuances. Using personal narratives and pop culture anecdotes, Farah walks readers through a journey to understand how to strengthen their emotional intelligence. Farah has a vast amount of experience and expertise, but it feels like she's speaking directly to the reader as a close friend. Anyone who wants to improve their relationships needs to pick up this book."

— Janice Gassam Asare,
Ph.D. DEI Consultant and Senior Contributing writer for *Forbes*

"Farah Harris has produced a timely and compelling book that creates a window into what happens inside many organizations and companies while also providing practical skills to understand and enhance emotional intelligence skills for leaders. Given the monumental gap in leadership in society, *The Color of Emotional Intelligence* is a vitally important and relevant read for leaders."

— Claude Robinson,
Founder/President of Onyx Strategic Partners, LLC.

THE
COLOR
OF
EMOTIONAL
INTELLIGENCE

ELEVATING OUR
SELF AND SOCIAL AWARENESS
TO ADDRESS INEQUITIES

FARAH HARRIS

Publishing support provided by
Ignite Press
5070 N. Sixth St. #189
Fresno, CA 93710
www.IgnitePress.us

ISBN: 979-8-9877639-0-2
ISBN: 979-8-9877639-1-9 (E-book)

For bulk purchases and for booking, contact:

Farah Harris
info@workingwelldaily.com
workingwelldaily.com

Library of Congress Control Number: 2023902283

Cover design by Rashmita Paul
Edited by Elizabeth Arterberry
Interior design by Jetlaunch

FIRST EDITION

DEDICATION

This book is for those who didn't realize that they were tired of showing up for everyone else but themselves because they thought this was the only way to live. For those who were hiding, presenting only shadows of themselves in places that falsely promoted authenticity.

To those who have been historically and systemically marginalized, traumatized, and aggressed, and, because of this, have learned survival skills that have unintentionally kept you bound—I hope that this book will free you up.

This book is for the diversity, equity, and inclusion practitioners who are exhausted because you, too, experience the microaggressions that the employees you serve are experiencing. You try to be the voice for the underrepresented, yet yours also gets quenched.

I see you. You are not alone. I pray this book lets you sit and catch your breath because you need to take care of yourself while doing this vital work. Emotionally intelligent self-care is key if you want to keep doing this in the long run.

This book is written for the leader who wants to be more courageous and curious with how to better support your employees—especially those from underrepresented groups.

May this book help you grow in awareness and give you the tools you need to lean into the discomfort that comes from becoming a great leader.

Finally, this book is written for all(ies) who want to show up and make a better world. I thank you.

TABLE OF CONTENTS

PART ONE:

EMOTIONAL INTELLIGENCE IN BLACK AND WHITE

1

WE DON'T SEASON OUR CHICKEN THE SAME

Are you a people-watcher like I am?

I've always been a people-watcher, curious about what made people tick and the stories behind their behavior. I didn't realize how much of an observer of human behavior I was until I shifted into the mental health field. When I considered the concept of emotional intelligence and its role in how we show up and manage relationships, it made me want to increase my emotional intelligence—also known as emotional quotient (EQ)—and help others do the same.

Far too many times, I've watched relationships struggle or fail due to poor communication or one person not being able to get a hold on their emotions. Similarly, I've sat through several boring presentations where the speaker seemed oblivious to participants' verbal and non-verbal cues. I think about all those meetings that could have been an email!

Quite frankly, I can't recall when I was first introduced to the concept of emotional intelligence. Was it through a book? An article? A podcast? I'm not sure. However, the moment emotional intelligence became known to me, it intuitively made sense. *Like, duh!* A competency that helps people better understand themselves and others by being more aware of what is going on internally and externally? *Sign me up!*

We'll delve into a more in-depth definition in Chapter 3, but, in short, *emotional intelligence is being able to manage your feelings and understand the emotions of those around you.*

When I received my graduate degree in mental health counseling, I knew I wanted to incorporate emotional intelligence into my clinical practice. Much of my work revolves around helping clients better process their thoughts and emotions, and the emotional intelligence skill works well with cognitive behavioral therapy and similar theoretical frameworks. Not only did I see its value as a therapeutic technique, but I also recognized its worth beyond the therapy couch, and even the corporate boardroom. This was a skill set everyone needed to improve their lives, to have a greater understanding of self, and to cultivate healthier relationships.

> **Yet, emotional intelligence is the most overhyped, underutilized, and misused skill that I can think of.**

Yet, emotional intelligence is the most overhyped, underutilized, and misused skill that I can think of.

It has become a trendy management buzzword that doesn't go into actual practice. As the saying goes, theory is great, but application is better. Many people know about emotional intelligence, but few practice what they know of it. Sarah Noll Wilson, leadership coach and author of *Don't Feed the Elephants,* points out, "There are many who know the concept of emotional intelligence intellectually, but I have seen few act intentionally with it."

The concept has become synonymous with high performance and leadership. That's all well and good; however, linking emotional intelligence solely to the workplace limits its application and approach. There's so much more to it. Emotional intelligence isn't a skill exclusively meant for professional development.

Does it benefit you in the professional arena? Absolutely! However, you must recognize that elevating your emotional intelligence is part of your personal development. It plays an essential role in how you live, see yourself, and interact with others. It takes courage, empathy, and effective communication beyond interpersonal skills. The better you can comprehend, grasp, and implement it, the more you recognize that it's not just a professional skill, but one that can improve your overall well-being.

It's also been disappointing to see it discussed primarily as a soft skill—there's nothing soft about it. Our emotional intelligence carries so much weight that it would be more aptly renamed a "strength skill." When we consider the work it takes to build and maintain healthy relationships in and out of the workplace and the resilience needed to navigate through difficult times, we realize that this skill isn't just nice to have, but *essential.*

The changes brought on during the Covid-19 pandemic challenged all of us. How did we respond to layoffs, working remotely, children attending school virtually, the Great Resignation (or as I prefer to call it, the Great Awakening), the steady waves of grief? We have needed extra doses of empathy, effective communication, vulnerability, and emotional regulation to maintain our well-being.

Does any of that sound like light work? Absolutely not. It takes strength to stay grounded and considerate while it seems like the world is unkind and unstable.

Perhaps you've been in a situation where you were doing your best to keep your cool and not explode on someone. Maybe it was a colleague who was working your last nerve. You were looking for that internal "whoosah."

Practicing this type of restraint consistently isn't easy. To those of you who are parents, I know that you feel me when I say parenting is not for the faint of heart. Our kids will try us, and we will lose it if we're not regulating ourselves! Slowing ourselves down to get our emotions under control and consider where the other person is coming from takes work!

This is why I call emotional intelligence a strength skill, because it can be difficult to stay emotionally regulated. Emotional intelligence is a vital muscle that needs continuous strength training, yet we consistently miss how this skill set is much deeper, broader, and richer than how it has been taught.

For years, the leading voices teaching us how to elevate our emotional intelligence have not included the historically underrepresented. Daniel Goleman, an internationally renowned psychologist, is known as the father of emotional intelligence. Along with Dr. Travis Bradberry and Stephen Covey, they are a few of the top voices. These thought leaders are predominantly White men.

Let's be clear, these professionals being White men isn't the issue; the problem is that their teaching, representation, and understanding comes from a limited perspective. For example, if you research heart disease and only use White males in the study, will the results of your study be wrong? Not exactly; it will be accurate for the represented group. However, those findings won't necessarily be relevant for or helpful to women or men of different ethnic backgrounds. What we want is something that isn't accurate in part. What we want is something more comprehensive.

There hasn't been much diversity in this space. As a Black woman, I offer a different perspective and understand that emotional intelligence is much more nuanced and robust than it's been presented to us. There has not been much consideration given to how inequity has impacted this skill set. Like many subjects, the current mainstream understanding of emotional intelligence is derived from a limited point of view, guided by those we consider experts based on their position in our society.

Have you ever wondered about those we deem experts and how often we've accepted their knowledge as the ultimate authority on a topic? We will implement a strategy or teach a subject matter without asking critical questions about whether the expert's conclusion is accurate, or whether it might be applicable to one group but not necessarily to another.

As a psychotherapist, this is a challenge that we face related to counseling theories, ethics, and the techniques we use in our practice. The way depression can present in someone from one culture may not be how it shows up in someone from another.

However, much of the theories and research in our field aren't diverse and inclusive. Therefore, the techniques taught to us are of limited use or inefficient for clients we serve who aren't White. We were given the same brush to use on them all. Can we actively serve our clients well when we try to make them fit into a box that was never designed for them?

When it comes to emotional intelligence, we must understand that we can be learning the same skill yet approaching it differently, because we are individuals with unique presuppositions, experiences, and abilities.

We cannot assume that we will all use emotional intelligence in the same way. Take cooking, for instance. Depending on where you live, a popular dish like pizza can be prepared in any great variety of ways. There's deep-dish, hand-tossed, flatbread, and thin crust. There are also many different ingredients that can be used to create unique and distinct flavors. Some may even argue that a particular region makes the best pizza. By the way, it's Chicago.

In 2006, on The Oprah Winfrey Show, Oprah taste-tests a chicken recipe that Anna Ginsberg submitted to a contest that won her a million-dollar prize.

After her first underwhelming bite, there's a long pause. Ginsberg asks Oprah, "Do you like it?"

Oprah continues to chew.

Ginsberg nervously tells Oprah, "Just say yes."

Oprah, measuring her words, says, ". . . Did we add salt and pepper? I think we needed salt and pepper."

You can see the surprise on Oprah's face when Anna tells her that salt and pepper weren't added. While the audience laughs, Oprah does her best to reaffirm to the cook that her chicken tastes good, but everyone could tell she was not a fan of the unseasoned chicken.

Let's face it, even something as basic as chicken is prepared differently based on cultural and socioeconomic upbringing. If we can approach cooking differently, we surely can approach a skill like emotional intelligence in distinctive ways.

Therefore, when we think about emotional intelligence, what are we not considering? In what ways do experiences of marginalization hone our intuition and soft skills? Does our identity as it relates to race, ethnicity, gender, sexuality, disability, age, and size intersect with or influence our emotional intelligence? Are there skills that enhance our emotional intelligence when dealing with folks who have underdeveloped or underutilized their emotional intelligence? How can emotional intelligence be used to foster a sense of belonging? These are just a few of the questions that we will process together.

Can I let you in on a secret? Those who have historically and systemically been marginalized use the competencies in this skill set differently and as a means of survival. However, before we go there, I want you to understand what emotional intelligence is in black and white before it is touched by color.

Oh! I might as well tell you right now; I will ask you many questions throughout this book because I want to help you slow down, critically think, and become more curious about your thoughts and feelings. I want you to practice emotional intelligence in real time while learning to understand yourself better and put on different frames to see others more clearly. Don't worry. I'll be with you every step of the way, helping you adjust your frames.

Pointing out areas you may have missed.

Turning you around when you want to avoid a concept.

Challenging your thoughts.

Affirming your feelings.

Slowing you down.

And sitting with you.

I know you're probably thinking, *Wait, what the heck am I about to get into?* Great! You've already started asking yourself questions and leading with curiosity!

Let's go walk the dog!

2

WALK THE DOG

"If you don't manage your emotions, they will manage you."

— Deborah Rozman

I live in a very dog-friendly community and have witnessed what seems like a dog walking its owner on more than one occasion. Yeah, I said what I said. I know you've seen it before. The dog dictates which way the owner should go—completely taking charge of this outdoor experience and testing how far they can extend their independence.

I had never considered that you need to train your dog to walk on a leash. I was naïve in thinking it was as simple as attaching the leash to the dog's collar, and off you go! Well, I was wrong.

Years ago, I watched an episode of *The Dog Whisperer*, where Cesar Millan, aka the "Dog Whisperer," taught his clients how to walk their dogs. He said to walk a dog properly, you don't want it to walk ahead of you because that means the dog is the pack leader and in control. You also don't want the dog to walk too far behind you. What you want is for the dog to walk alongside you. This way, you can properly engage with it. You can see it, guide it, and remain in control.

I immediately thought this was a perfect metaphor to describe emotional intelligence! Specifically, it is relevant to the domains of self-awareness and self-management.

What does it look like when your emotions run ahead of you and have more control of you than you have of them? It seems like you're going from zero to one hundred in an instant! However, this isn't to say that you're always quick to anger; it could mean that you often make snap decisions and act on how you feel in the moment without considering other factors. In other words, you act impulsively.

At the same time, you also don't want your emotions behind you, because you won't be able to see what's coming—and neither will anyone else. When this happens, you can come across as being passive or passive-aggressive. You may present like everything's fine, but in reality, you're angry or disappointed.

We want to be in lockstep with our emotions—being fully present, aware of them, and experiencing them in real-time. In essence, we want to make sure that we are not just keeping our emotions on a leash but that we know what kind of dog, aka emotion, we are walking with. You may think you're walking with anger when, actually, it's guilt or shame.

I watch how our children manage vulnerable emotions. Sometimes they do it well, and other times, not so much. Our oldest often will lead with anger when he's called out on unkind behavior to his younger sister. It never fails; the two of them will begin play-fighting and I will hear them laughing one minute, followed by, "Ouch! That hurts."

"Oh my gosh! No, it doesn't!"

"Yes! That hurt!"

"You're just saying that so Mommy can hear you."

To which my daughter exclaims, "No, that really hurt."

By the time I've entered the room, I can see in his face and hear in his words that he's upset. After he's calmed down, I ask him if it's possible that he wasn't angry with his sister or me, but more so that he didn't like that his actions caused harm.

I do my best to highlight that he's not paying attention to his dog. Being aware of his true feelings can help him move out of discomfort more quickly by acknowledging the wrong, which can help to expedite reconciliation between him and his sister. We're still working on it. It's a process.

Some of us can identify our emotions only after the moment has passed. In hindsight, we can pinpoint why we reacted the way we did. Having emotional intelligence helps us decrease the gap between awareness and the moment. You can learn to do this by practicing the three A's:

- Aware(ness)
- Assess(ment)
- Address/Action

Aware(ness)

Have you ever had a lump form in your throat right before having to share some difficult news? Do you realize that you are clenching your teeth and balling up your fists when someone crosses you? That's your body telling you that you're nervous or angry. When feelings come up for you, can you name them? Awareness allows you to notice and name your feelings in real time. To do this, you need to practice the pause. Slow yourself down. Try taking a deep breath. Okay, what are you feeling? Is it anger? Anxiety? Joy? Sadness?

The more in tune we are with our bodies, the greater our awareness will be as our bodies help us identify what we are feeling.

Also, putting a label on your emotion can create some distance from it and possibly decrease the intensity of the feeling. Some people have a significant emotional vocabulary and high emotional literacy, making the identifying and naming of their emotions easier. Increasing your emotional vocabulary can aid you in naming your emotions more quickly.

Assess(ment)

After you've put a name to how you're feeling, you need to keep holding that pause button so you can assess the source of this feeling. Are you angry because someone cut you off on the way to the office? Did you just get wind of the news that you won a free trip, so you're excited? Was there a sudden noise that is now making you anxious? Are you sad because the anniversary of a loved one's passing is coming up?

Like "Track Changes" on a Word document, you need to track the origin of your feelings to identify the reason you're experiencing this emotional response. Being able to assess gives us time to understand our present state better and begin a plan of action as to our next steps.

If you think you can skip this step, you are wrong. Going straight from awareness to action is an impulsive response. We want to learn to slow our brains down long enough to develop a rational response. We will get more into this in Chapter 5. Trust me, holding down that pause button saves you from looking and acting foolish.

We see many people being challenged with this stage of slowing down in everyday situations. They feel their feelings so strongly that they believe they are making the right decision to go out with a person or purchase an expensive item without taking the time to assess the situation.

They disregard the red flags and caution signs until after they've been burned. I've known people who quickly dove into problematic relationships and became the butt of their friends' jokes or pitied by their peers because they moved from feeling to action too soon.

In early 2001, one of my best friends desperately wanted to buy a Cadillac Catera. He instantly fell in love with it and ignored the warnings his father and others gave him. As a recent college graduate, he wanted to prove that he was "grown" and could make his own decisions.

Throwing wise counsel out the window, he purchased the car. It didn't take long for the car to start having issue after issue. His pride got the best of him; he rushed in and made a poor (and expensive) decision. Trust me, there's a blessing in the pause. Our emotions can be deceitful. If we take time to assess our feelings and be honest with ourselves, it can prevent us from taking ill-informed action.

By the way, they stopped production of the Catera in the same year my friend purchased his.

Address/Action

Once you understand the *what* and the *why*, you can move on to the *how*. What must we consider as the best course of action to address a given situation in a way that will serve you and others well? This means determining what can help decrease conflict and not create more issues.

Giving yourself time to breathe and reflect helps to minimize reactive behavior. How many of us have sent an email too soon and regretted not slowing ourselves down to respond in a more measured and controlled manner? Maybe you've accused someone of wrongdoing before having all of the facts. There's wisdom in learning how to be quick to listen, slow to speak, and slow to become angry.

Reacting is being led by our emotions. Responding is being led by our thoughts.

Reacting is being led by our emotions. Responding is being led by our thoughts.

Being able to understand why you feel the way you do and slowing yourself down long enough to regulate your emotions sets you up to respond in a calm and collected manner. Practicing the three A's helps increase your self-awareness and emotional awareness while learning to better manage and regulate your feelings. The pause also allows you to not only be curious about your thoughts and emotions, but also to consider what the other person may be thinking and feeling.

I doubt you will ever look at dog-walking in the same way. Whenever you see someone walking their dog, or maybe whenever you're walking your own, I hope you think about emotional intelligence and ask yourself, *Are my emotions walking me, or am I walking with them?*

-EQ REVIEW-

- Managing and controlling our emotions is similar to walking a dog.

- You don't want your emotions to lead you from the front or lag behind; instead, you want them to walk alongside you.

- The three A's of emotional intelligence are:

  o   Aware(ness) - Naming your feelings and practicing the pause.

  o   Assess(ment) - Analyzing the origin of your feelings.

  o   Action/Address - Action helps you address your emotions in a way that will serve you and others well.

- Practicing "the three A's" helps increase your self-awareness and emotional awareness while learning to better manage and regulate your feelings, which will help you experience less stress and cultivate healthy relationships.

3

DOMAINS OF EMOTIONAL INTELLIGENCE

"Between stimulus and response, there's space. In that space lies our freedom and power to choose our response. In our response lies growth and freedom."

— Viktor E. Frankl

Emotional intelligence is defined as the act of knowing, understanding, and responding to emotions within yourself and others. It is also the ability to be aware of how your words and actions affect those around you. Or, simply, it's the ability to be in tune with yourself and your emotions and to be able to "read the room."

This skill set comprises of four domains: self-awareness, self-management, social awareness, and relationship management. Within these domains are competencies such as emotional awareness, adaptability, empathy, and effective communication, to name a few.

Let's walk through these stepping stones that make up the framework of emotional intelligence.

Self-Awareness

There was a smack heard around the world. It came from the hand of actor Will Smith on the night of the 2022 Oscars. Smith got up from his chair in the audience, went on stage, and slapped comedian Chris Rock across the face. At first, viewers and those present wondered if it was scripted. It wasn't. When Smith returned to his seat, he angrily cursed at Rock, warning him to keep his wife's, Jada Pinkett-Smith's, name out of his mouth.

Before the altercation, Rock had jokingly asked Jada when the next G.I. Jane movie was coming out. It was in reference to her recently shaved head. Whether or not he knew that Jada suffered from alopecia, which causes hair loss, doesn't matter. It was a poor joke. However, Smith's reaction didn't match the situation. Sans the slap, Smith made it clear with his words what he was not going to accept from Rock. Matching words with words would have been sufficient. But he went beyond words. He chose to assault someone.

Surprisingly, Smith was allowed to remain at the ceremony, and the Academy Awards continued without a hitch. Moments after assaulting Rock, Smith went on stage to accept his award and offered an emotional speech and apology.

When you watch the entire situation unfold, you can see many emotional layers to this. If you followed the media frenzy around it, it was easy to see how divided people were regarding the whole matter. It was startling to see how many approved of Smith's behavior and viewed it as chivalrous. However, examining his words, behavior, and emotions before and after the altercation, you can see that his actions even took him by surprise.

In 2021, Will Smith released his autobiography, which detailed his childhood trauma from living in an abusive home with an alcoholic father. This included experiences which led him to question his masculinity and what it looks like to protect the women in his life when he could not defend his mother from his father's brutal blows. These emotional narratives, a subject we will discuss later in Chapter 6, are what simmers beneath this type of behavior.

When our emotional reactions don't match a situation, more than likely, we lack self-awareness. In the previous chapter, we addressed how when we experience intense emotions and allow them to take over, we are no longer walking the dog. While the event may be the trigger, our response is usually the result of something more than what is presently happening. What was witnessed at the Academy Awards was an overflow of emotional lava that singed the remainder of what was supposed to be a celebratory night.

Self-awareness is the bedrock of emotional intelligence, from which all other competencies can flow. It involves being aware of our feelings, motives, beliefs, and desires. It also helps us understand our strengths and weaknesses and why we do what we do.

Oddly enough, you must have some amount of self-awareness to want to become more self-aware. The journey we take to self-discovery isn't a smooth ride. There are prickly moments, times where we stumble, and situations that can delay us or propel us forward. To be able to recognize our behaviors is a process. Sometimes, it's a difficult and painful one.

Learning of self requires you to take inventory of all the things that shape you.

You didn't just wake up like this. We are a sum of our parts. We may want to dismiss our histories, but ignoring pieces of ourselves doesn't allow us to see the whole picture. According to research conducted by Dr. Tasha Eurich, 95% of people think they're self-aware, while only 10-15% truly are. She says, "That means, on a good day, about 80 percent of people are lying about themselves—to themselves."

Some may be aware of their poor behavior, yet they use excuses that masquerade as self-awareness. Proclamations such as "Well, you know I'm hot-tempered" or "I'm always fashionably late" may be used to justify their behavior, but if they aren't going to do anything to change it, then what's the point? Don't just proclaim your short-comings; ask yourself why they are short. Knowledge may not be enough to change behavior. However, the possession of knowledge does entail responsibility.

> **To be ignorant or naïve is one thing, but to know something about yourself that negatively impacts others (or yourself) and do nothing to change it is irresponsible.**

To be ignorant or naïve is one thing, but to know something about your-self that negatively impacts others (or yourself) and do nothing to change it is irresponsible.

Emotional Awareness

To be self-aware is also to practice emotional awareness. When we feel our feelings, emotional awareness allows us to be aware of and name the emotion. However, our emotional vocabulary can be limited by our upbringing. This means that we can feel an emotion without quite knowing how to name it, if we weren't taught how.

In the first chapter of the book, *The Giver*, Jonas, the main character, is determined to find the right word to describe his feelings. As a young boy, he was careful with language and wanted to ensure that he used accurate wording when communicating. His family practiced a daily ritual every evening, a "telling of feelings."

After they finished their dinner, Jonas' father would ask, "Who wants to be first tonight for feelings?"

Then, one by one, each member of the family would share how they were feeling and what made them feel that way. Everyone would listen to each other, ask for clarification, provide input, and validate each other's feelings. So many of us would have benefited from this daily exercise.

What emotion am I feeling right now? How does it feel in my body? How might this other person experience my emotion?

Sometimes, we add an emotion on top of an emotion. We're angry because we're anxious. We'll say, "I can't believe I'm letting this get to me!" This can cause us to inadvertently add unnecessary judgment and derails and delays us from addressing the initial emotion.

When we ask ourselves what is behind our feelings, we can get to the real story. Are we angry? Or are we embarrassed, fearful, sad, or disappointed? Anger is often a secondary emotion. Unearthing the true feeling can take some work that some are unwilling to do, typically because they do not have the tools or they're avoiding an uncomfortable truth.

Being able to shift from judgment to reflection can help us assess where the feeling came from and then decide how we want to respond. This is how we self-audit and take inventory to be better stewards of ourselves. For those of us who have been harmed so much, our pain can obscure our awareness. We will discuss more how our trauma can be a barrier to exercising our EQ in Chapter 7.

To fully practice self-awareness requires vulnerability and openness to ask another person how they perceive us. It's a two-sided coin: on one side, it's how we experience ourselves—recognizing our thoughts, emotions, behaviors, strengths, and weaknesses—and, on the other, it's awareness of how others experience us.

However, when we go deeper and move from theory to practice, requesting feedback and engaging in the self-auditing exercise of asking ourselves the necessary questions, it helps us understand the "why we do what we do" behind the "who we are."

Feedback

"I'll never forget when we were in college, and you told me that I had an anger problem."

My childhood friend, Eric, said this to me during one of our lengthy phone conversations.

"You told me that this 'rage issue' was something I needed to be more accountable for. I knew instinctively that you were sharing something important, but I didn't have access to break it down at that time. I just trusted what you were saying on a base level; this [anger] thing wasn't good for me. . . I didn't ask myself the questions about how, why, and where did this come from? You know, getting to the root of it. I didn't know any of that. I just took it as, 'Well, you need to stop doing that and slow down because this isn't good for you.'"

This recollection seems to come up a few times a year during our phone calls. I clearly remember the day I shared with Eric, this feedback about his anger. It was after he had come over to vent about a recent conflict with his roommate that had upset him. I watched and listened as he explained his side of the story.

"I can't believe he didn't wake me up!"

I watched as his face turned red and he began to seethe.

"Wait, you're mad because you turned off your alarm and your roommate didn't wake you up so that you could make it to class?" I asked, confused.

"Yes!" He screamed, proceeding to call his roommate every name in the book.

As he spoke, I recognized that his reaction to this situation wasn't unique; in fact, it was becoming increasingly familiar. The intensity of his emotional response didn't match the offense. An air of self-righteous indignation and something else I couldn't put my finger on eclipsed his ability to see and respond rationally. He was completely unaware of his behavior and the potential harm it could cause him and others. I was concerned that there would be consequences and repercussions if he didn't become more aware.

When we consider improving our self-awareness, we view it as a solo activity. However, if we are not careful to ask for feedback, our picture of ourselves will not be accurate. Even an artist who sketches a self-portrait needs the assistance of a mirror. To see ourselves correctly, we need feedback.

"Self-awareness is convenient when comfortable," shares leadership coach Sarah Noll Wilson. "So often how it's understood and put into practice is to reinforce a level of comfort."

This comfort level contributes to maintaining our blind spots and feeding our cognitive dissonance. Our egos are a pretty delicate thing. They can get bruised easily; therefore, we avoid feedback and would prefer to skip it altogether—who truly enjoys being critiqued? However, asking someone you consider trustworthy to provide constructive criticism and honest feedback can help you better understand how others experience you and how your behavior impacts them.

Looking in the mirror is not a comfortable exercise. It's an activity that we would rather not do because it involves us facing the truth of who we are. Lean into courage and vulnerability and take more than just a glance. Really look at yourself. What habits do you have that help you or harm you? Permit yourself to observe how you show up, think, and feel throughout the day.

When we lack self-awareness, we fail to identify what we're feeling and how it affects our daily actions. We don't see the patterns in how we think and behave, which causes us to make excuses for our behavior.

Lack of self-awareness also makes it challenging to set boundaries, therefore giving more space to people and activities that increase our negative emotions. By elevating the competency of our self-awareness, we can decrease unnecessary stressors caused by us not being aligned with our choices and desires.

Consistent practice of self-awareness will encourage you to be more mindful and gather emotional and cognitive feedback to help guide your days and decision-making. The more aware you are of *who* you are, the more authentically you will be able to show up in the world.

Self-Management

There's an episode of *Divorce Court* with Judge Lynn Toler where a woman hummed every time her ex-husband spoke. She would melodically moan if she didn't like what was said. When his mistress entered the courtroom and began to speak, the volume of her humming increased, and she'd start to sing her rebuttals. Of course, the judge asked her to stop because it was disruptive. The woman then stated that she hummed to help her regulate her anger and that it was a coping mechanism she learned from her anger management classes and her therapist.

You could tell that this woman was a singer, and she used what was natural to her to help her in stressful situations. You may not have the gift of singing, but I encourage you to find ways to manage your emotions, like going for a walk, counting to ten (or for some of you, a hundred), listening to music, exercising, meditation, or prayer.

I believe if self-management were a person, they'd rock a t-shirt quoting rapper Ice Cube, with "Check yourself before you wreck yourself" written across the chest in big red letters. Self-management is being disciplined and self-controlled and taking responsibility for your behavior.

It's here that we practice the pause. We not only try to find our inner zen, but we also examine ourselves by self-auditing to process our feelings. Once again, a reminder that this process is done without judgment but with curiosity. Managing our emotions decreases the chances that they will overwhelm us and spur us to act in ways that produce negative consequences. It is this skill that allows us to manage our stress better.

We can see the absence of self-management frequently on social media. People will read a post or see a clip and immediately have something to say. Often, they are loud and wrong! Have you ever read a comment under a post, scratched your head, and thought, "Did we read the same thing?"

The poster quickly responded without taking time to carefully read or watch the media and fully process their feelings on it before responding. Sometimes it's something within the post that is triggering. Other times, we can be reactive because of non-related factors impacting our patience and comprehension. Are we too tired? Are we already overwhelmed? Maybe we're just hungry—there's much truth in those Snicker commercials. Whatever it is, there are always opportunities for us to slow ourselves down and pump the breaks before we wreck ourselves.

Poor self-management makes it difficult for us to handle stress effectively. It can cause us to behave destructively, leading us to addictions, ranging from drugs to retail therapy. This impulsivity can negatively impact our relationships through our lack of discipline and inability to regulate our feelings.

The more we can increase our ability to self-regulate, the less we will have to deal with regret. When we don't practice self-management, it is challenging to empathize and be patient, which are needed to learn the following two skills of social awareness and relationship management.

Social Awareness

Have you ever had a conversation with someone and realized that she wasn't listening to a word you were saying mid-way through? It's as if you are talking to a wall. Or perhaps you've attended an event, and the speaker is so enthralled with his story that he didn't see, or maybe he didn't care, that several audience members had begun to scroll on their phones, fidget uncomfortably in their seats, or have hushed conversations amongst themselves.

I think back to when I was a little girl sitting in church, hearing some parishioners begin to use their "amen" in a strategic way to end what was perceived as a long and unenlightening message.

The preacher would speak. The congregation would say "Amen."

He'd continue. They'd say amen a little louder.

As the sermon dragged on, the amens became more frequent and increased in volume.

Even as a kid, I could tell there was a difference between an amen of agreement and one of annoyance. What they were doing was the latter. They were trying to politely tell the preacher to sit down and shut up, but, you know, in the King James Version.

Our words, behaviors, and expressions of emotion must align with what is happening around us. Imagine hearing some exciting news that you can't wait to share with your colleague. You head straight to her office, but you see several coworkers with their heads down and appearing somber upon your arrival. It turns out that there was a terrible accident nearby, and there were fatalities. Is this the best time to share your announcement? Do you take a moment to assess the situation and decide that this news would be best shared later?

Social awareness is the ability to see the perspectives of another person, group, or community and apply that understanding to guide your interaction with them. It's being able to identify verbal and non-verbal social cues. It's also how we manage our emotions in social situations so that we respond appropriately. It's within this domain that we see empathy at play. I like to say that this domain is the ability to read the room—and care.

Social awareness is remembering that it isn't all about you, that there are other people's feelings that you must consider. Take a moment to read the room, whether it be a physical or virtual space. Learn to adjust yourself to ensure that your emotional response matches the environment. Your emotions and behaviors affect others.

The above illustrations could be seen as minor instances of low social awareness. However, a lack of social awareness can have significant negative impacts, especially when it involves persons or groups experiencing grief or loss or those from underrepresented backgrounds.

Certain holidays like Mother's Day or Father's Day are days of celebration for many, but for others, these days are filled with grief: the grief of losing a parent, child, or the memory of toxic relationships of abuse or neglect. Do you take a moment to consider those who may be dealing with multiple losses on those days? They may be mourning the loss of their parent (or parents), and the space unfilled by a child they weren't able to have or one they couldn't keep on this side of Heaven.

When I was growing up, there was a saying, "This is an A B conversation, so C your way out."

It often was said when someone tried to interject their thoughts and presence in a conversation that didn't pertain to them. Because our conversations are now both on and offline, this social awareness isn't limited to the physical space.

Many conversations online are specific to a particular group, yet you will frequently find someone who adds their comment, not considering those whom they are addressing. It can sometimes derail the conversation or, worse, gaslight others. It matters not the intention but more so the impact.

When a group of Black people shares how something is affecting them, there will always be someone who isn't Black who thinks it's their place to insert their opinion. For example, there was a Black woman who shared her experience of her pain being dismissed after childbirth due to systemic racism and a White woman interjected, saying that her nurses didn't want to give her pain medication either after she delivered her baby.

Are you familiar with the term *mansplaining*? This is when a man explains something to a woman in a belittling and condescending way. A woman can express frustration regarding an experience that many women encounter, and inevitably, there will be a man who feels he must tell her "not all men," or that what she's describing is not what she is claiming it to be. It's tiring, and the lack of social awareness of others can cause us to feel unsafe and restricted in how we express ourselves.

Our world is diverse. Being socially aware helps us to interact with people from different backgrounds. It helps us to come alongside others and empathize. It can be hurtful when we feel unseen, as if our experiences, thoughts, and feelings don't matter. Increasing our social awareness helps us understand each other's perspectives, making it easier to regulate emotions and better communicate. It helps us to respond to the needs of others and, ideally, for others to respond to our needs.

Relationship Management

Imagine getting fired over Zoom. That was the experience of nine hundred Better.com employees in early December 2021. In less than 5 minutes, a CEO rocked the world of 900 people and found a way to make the whole thing about him. In his video where the chat feature was disabled, he stated that the layoff was a hard decision but ultimately up to him.

Although the decision was his to make, it's best to explain the reason behind it to those who are impacted by the decision when practicing relationship management. Under this domain, we can find effective communication, team building, conflict management, influence, and collaboration competencies. It appears that these may not have been considered before the initiation of this layoff.

To effectively communicate, one must use the awareness of their emotions and those of others to manage interactions successfully. In essence, utilizing the strategies of self-awareness, self-management, and social awareness is the three-pronged approach necessary to successfully develop your relationship management skills.

This CEO's decision to mute attendees and ignore the chat was a clear example of conflict avoidance. He was looking to find ways to make it easy for him while delivering a difficult announcement. There wasn't much consideration or empathy given to the employees. Instead of delivering the message with compassion, he made his brief announcement more about himself than his staff.

The poor execution of this layoff was shared in many articles, where writers and readers both criticized the CEO's actions. He later apologized and took some time off to reflect and conduct a "leadership and cultural assessment." You would have thought that the criticism would have provided him with the necessary feedback needed to correct the current course; however, three months later, the company again had a mass layoff of 3000 employees. The staff received their severance checks before receiving a formal notice. You can't make this stuff up.

It may not be an uncaring boss, but you may know someone that makes having a fruitful relationship challenging. It would be nice to like and get along with every person we meet, but that's not our reality. Sometimes, the challenge can come from our family members or friends. Maybe it's managing a relationship with a parent who's an alcoholic, or perhaps it's figuring out ways to communicate better what you desire from your partner.

Whether we want to admit it or not, relationships play a significant role in our lives. The better we manage them, the more we can increase our well-being.

Unless you live alone on a remote island, you are bound to interact and engage with other people. Fostering value-added relationships is key to navigating everyday interactions and maintaining long-term relationships. It's always admirable when someone can stay composed and confident in difficult situations.

Managing our emotions can help us manage our relationships better. When we're involved in an emotionally charged conflict, this is not the time to match the other person's energy. This can add fuel to the fire, and if we're not careful, everyone will get burned.

I think about when a child throws a tantrum or when an older child behaves in a way we believe is disrespectful. Losing our cool doesn't help simmer things down. What generally happens is that we end up creating more distance between ourselves and the child or having what was annoying whining become a full-blown meltdown.

Relationship management is designed to help you:

1. **Communicate Effectively**: You are able to engage assertively. Passivity or passive-aggressive communication is a sign of low emotional intelligence. Learning how to communicate in a non-defensive way will help avoid aggressive, passive, or passive-aggressive behaviors.

2. **Give and receive feedback**: It isn't easy to share feedback that can be perceived as negative. Providing constructive and respectful feedback helps minimize the threat or fear threshold, which minimizes your own and others' negative reactions that trigger fight-flight-freeze responses.

3. **Manage conflict**: You can approach disagreements calmly and respectfully. You intentionally create a welcoming environment for conversation by actively listening and seeking to find

common ground. Also, you are proactive in addressing poor behavior instead of being conflict-avoidant and allowing the poor behavior to go unchecked.

4. **Influence and motivate others**: When others see us practicing our emotional intelligence well, they will desire to emulate the same behavior—creating a positive atmosphere that will win the support of others because they feel seen, heard, and respected by you.

Emotional intelligence isn't a skill with a clear finish line or a pinnacle. Your emotional intelligence gets tested. Life gives you opportunities to use emotional intelligence wisely and effectively. You aren't always going to respond with high EQ. You may be able to regulate yourself during an intense negotiation for work, then later lose your patience during a conversation with your partner. None of us are perfect, so there may be times when we'll be able to execute these competencies successfully, and in the next instance, we might falter.

Now that we have learned about the domains of emotional intelligence, let's take a look at what goes on in the brain when we are experiencing our feelings.

-EQ REVIEW-

- Self-awareness is the bedrock from which other EQ competencies can flow.

- Self-awareness involves being aware of your feelings, motives, beliefs, and desires.

- Self-management is being disciplined, self-controlled, and taking responsibility for your behavior.

- Social awareness is the ability to see another person's, group's, or community's perspective and apply that understanding to guide your interaction with them. It's being able to identify verbal and non-verbal social cues. It's also how we manage our emotions in social situations to respond appropriately.

- Relationship management is designed to help you communicate effectively, give and receive feedback, manage conflict, and to influence and motivate others.

- Relationships play a significant role in our lives. Therefore, it is best to manage them well to improve our well-being.

- Emotional intelligence isn't a skill with a clear finish line or a pinnacle. Life will continue to create opportunities for you to use emotional intelligence wisely and effectively.

4

A BIT OF NEUROSCIENCE

"If you give in to your emotion, you lose yourself. You must be at one with your emotions because the body always follows the mind."

— *Bruce Lee*

Riley is an eleven-year-old girl who moves from Minnesota to San Francisco because of her father's job. Trying to adjust to her new world isn't easy, and her once happy-go-lucky personality shifts to become moodier and more frustrated. Her emotions are led by Joy, who tries to help her navigate this difficult time. However, the stress of all the changes brings Sadness to the forefront. However, when Joy and Sadness get sucked out of the Headquarters to the recesses of Riley's mind, only Fear, Anger, and Disgust are left to take over.

This is the plot of Pixar's movie, *Inside Out*—a brilliant movie that teaches how the brain processes emotions. Albeit an animated film marketed to children, it is one that I often recommend to my therapy clients. Watching cute cartoon characters that represent our emotions allows even adult viewers to explore the complexity of their feelings in a simplistic way.

There's so much happening in our brains that we don't realize. However, the more we learn about and recognize how it functions, the better we can optimize it. The brain is the most extraordinary computer there is! It has always fascinated me how it takes in information, manipulates it, and then chooses outputs. As humans, we experience, on average, 70,000 thoughts each day. How well are you mining and regulating those thoughts?

The nerd in me loves adding a little neuroscience wherever I can. So, let's look at what's happening in that head of yours!

The limbic system is the part of the brain specializing in our physical, emotional, and psychological responses. It's made up of three regions: the hippocampus (which deals with our memories), the amygdala (which deals with our emotions), and the hypothalamus (which deals with our internal regulation). We will focus only on the amygdala, the headquarters of these wonderful emotional characters, to keep it simple.

Our limbic system is connected to our brainstem. This is also known as our lower brain or "survival brain." It is the most primitive part of the brain, and it regulates specific involuntary actions of the body— for example, our heart rate, blood pressure, breathing, eating, reflexes, and sleeping.

When the amygdala is triggered, it signals to the brainstem that there's a threat and activates the fight-flight-freeze response, or, as I call them, Charlie's Angels. These two parts like to communicate to keep us alive. Back in the day when we were protecting ourselves from lions, tigers, and bears (oh my!), we needed these regions to respond quickly for our survival.

Although we no longer have to navigate unpredictable environments, our brain still watches out for real or perceived threats. It may not be a bear staring you down, but your supervisor; nevertheless, your brain might react the same way. Perhaps when you hear the words "we need to talk" from your partner, your amygdala gets activated.

We are now in the twenty-first century. Our brains are still evolving, and it's not until age twenty-five that our brains are fully formed. The development of the brain begins from the bottom up, or, some may say, from back to front. Therefore, the part of your brain which controls reasoning, logic, and common sense is the last to develop.

Think back to all those stupid mistakes you made in your youth. Now it's all beginning to make sense. For that reason, let's give our adolescents some grace. They're not working with a full tank.

This most evolved part of the brain is called our Prefrontal Cortex (PFC). It's the CEO of your brain. In keeping with the Charlie's Angels theme, you can call it Charlie. Our planning, decision-making, self-control, and problem-solving take place here. Our prefrontal cortex uses up a lot of energy; therefore, we must learn to manage this brain function well.

Now that we know our three main parts, the PFC, amygdala, and the brainstem, how do they function when we practice emotional intelligence?

Imagine drawing a line from your brain stem, working your way up through your limbic system, and, finally, to your PFC. That's how many of us utilize our brain—taking a low-high approach. We feel, we react, and then we think over our behavior.

Our brainstem and our limbic system are connected. The problem is that we often let these two parts seize our brains. It's as if our emotions have taken control, pressing all the buttons in the command center and saying, "I am the captain now!"

However, when we implement the pause and take a deep breath, which allows the necessary oxygen and blood to flow to our brains, it helps move us from our feeling brain to our thinking brain. In that way, we can respond more rationally, logically, and reasonably, taking the time to ask ourselves questions like,

"What about this is making me angry?"

"What evidence is there to warrant this fear?"

High emotional intelligence takes a high-low approach to using our brains. The PFC and the amygdala do more of the communicating so you can address the situation in a controlled manner without those Angels having us fighting, fleeing, or freezing unnecessarily.

When they're hijacking, we respond and do everything based on how we're feeling without communicating with our thinking brain.

Many times, it's a trauma response. Our brains go on autopilot, and we act before we think. We want to use our EQ effectively and have the CEO of our brain take the lead and say, "Hey, I understand that you're angry right now, but let's think things through. Could there be a better way to handle this?"

Why This Matters

The more we understand how our brains process emotions, the better we can *control* our emotions. Doing so will help us manage our responses, especially in stressful situations.

-EQ REVIEW-

- When understanding how our brain processes emotions, we can look at three main areas: the amygdala, the brainstem, and the prefrontal cortex.

- The amygdala is the feeling brain and is in the limbic system.

- The brainstem is the most primitive part of our brain and is our automatic control center.

- The prefrontal cortex (PFC) is the most evolved part of the brain and isn't fully developed until around age twenty-five.

- The PFC is our thinking brain and helps formulate reasonable and logical responses.

- Low emotional intelligence is when we allow our feeling brain and survival brain to take over.

- Practicing high emotional intelligence is when we intentionally activate our prefrontal cortex.

5

EMPATHY AND THE ROLE EMOTIONS PLAY

"Could a greater miracle take place than for us to look through each other's eye for an instant?"

—*Henry David Thoreau*

"Mommy, is he sad?"

I recall my oldest asking these questions when he was a preschooler. We'd watch television together, and he'd have a quizzical look whenever a character began expressing certain emotions. It didn't matter if the character was animated or a real actor; he genuinely was curious about what they were feeling.

My oldest is now a preteen, and one of his favorite courses is his social-emotional class. I recently discovered that he had found a couple of YouTube channels dedicated to social-emotional learning. Together, with his younger sister, we've watched a few videos and shared our takeaways. It's important, as a parent, that my children learn to understand their emotions and those of others so that they can begin practicing emotional intelligence and grow their empathy for others.

Emotions are data. They play an essential role in how we engage with the world and one another. They aren't random, rather, they provide us with the necessary information to help us respond to and learn from our experiences.

Think back to when you were a child. Maybe you touched a hot iron, or perhaps you slammed your finger in the door. You learned quickly not to handle the iron when it was on and became careful when closing doors. Through these incidents, the data you received helped you recall that being inattentive with those objects would bring pain.

This data provides us with the feedback needed to know what brings us joy or frustrates us. We feel positive emotions when we are around certain people or when we participate in a particular activity. We also feel unpleasant emotions when engaging in specific tasks or with certain individuals. Our emotions can help us improve our self-care when we pay attention to what they tell us.

Our brain collects facts and feelings and stores our experiences. In the movie *Inside Out*, we see how Riley's memories are associated with a particular emotion. As the film progresses, we see how core memories can be infused with more than one emotion. Joy works feverishly to keep Riley's memories happy but comes to realize that Sadness is needed for Riley's mental health.

Sometimes our experiences and memories bring both joy and sadness. This can happen when we think of a loved one who has since passed on, or maybe a season of your life that you look back on fondly. Knowing that you can't return to these times can leave you feeling bittersweet or nostalgic.

Emotions aren't finite. They are like writings in the sand. Before we know it, a wave can wash away the very feeling we thought was so permanent and leave our banks clear of whatever once was there. Feelings are fleeting. They are real, but they are not always accurate.

You can be furious that a friend is late in picking you up. You told them that you needed to get to a particular location at a specific time and mustn't be late. Then you receive a call from your friend letting you know that they've been in an accident and are hurt. Immediately your feelings shift from anger to concern and fear.

Emotions give us the drive to act. Once your brain acknowledges that something can cause harm, you will act in ways to avoid it. For example, when you see the danger of an oncoming car, the emotional response you have is fear, which speaks to your body and tells it to press on the brakes or to turn the steering wheel.

Emotions also help us interpret other people's feelings. As I shared earlier, my son was trying to understand what emotions the actors and characters were trying to convey. The more accurate we become in interpreting someone's feelings, the better we are at empathizing and responding accordingly.

Empathy is an emotional intelligence competency. It's the ability to understand what another person is experiencing from their point of reference. However, there is more than one type of empathy. Psychologists have identified three types of empathy: cognitive, emotional, and compassionate.

Cognitive empathy is the practice of understanding what a person might be thinking. It's comprehension on an intellectual level. People who are good at making sales have learned the art of cognitive empathy to anticipate what a potential buyer could be thinking. They play to their emotions to encourage them to buy the product or service they are providing.

It's a skill that also works well when negotiating and trying different perspectives. It is an excellent skill to have, but due to it being more about understanding someone's thoughts than their feelings, those who respond to others in this way can come off as cold or detached.

You might have experienced this after receiving a surprising diagnosis. The doctor quickly addressed your initial questions; however, they did not have the patience to dive into the emotions that come up for you.

Emotional empathy is when you physically feel what the other person is going through. You might be familiar with the term "empath," used to describe someone who is highly attuned to the mental and emotional state of those around them. When they feel, they feel deeply.

The downside to this type of empathy is that you can quickly burn out because it is hard to separate yourself from another person's distress. Feeling all the feelings all of the time can bring about a certain level of exhaustion. Therefore, implementing emotional boundaries is necessary.

Finally, *compassionate empathy* requires us to understand a person's experience and encourages us to try to help. This type of empathy requires us to think, feel, and act. It considers the whole person, honoring the connection between head and heart. Compassionate empathy recognizes what a person could be feeling while also considering the situation from an intellectual standpoint and having a healthy boundary that doesn't allow you to lose your center or autonomy.

This has been the role that many therapists play with their clients. As a therapist, I listen to my clients' predicaments, clarifying what they are thinking and feeling and doing my best to come alongside to help and comfort them, but without getting entangled in their experience.

I'm frequently asked how I am not more affected by my work. Part of it is personality, and the other part is practice. I learned early on to implement healthy emotional boundaries. My clients' lives are their own, and I have my own life to be present in. I cannot go home with their issues or take their stuff into the next session with another client.

It's as if whenever I provide therapy, I am entering an apartment building, with each unit representing a client. Once I finish my session, I close the door to one apartment and enter the next. At the end of the day, I leave the building to go to my residence, leaving my clients to keep their issues.

There's a healthy way to balance using emotional intelligence to offer genuine compassion while maintaining autonomy and loving detachment. It's not an easy feat to hold space for others. Therefore, we practice cognitive or emotional empathy because it's easier for many to lean to one side based on our comfort level.

Because empathy is a competency within emotional intelligence, we often believe that a person practicing emotional intelligence will be an empathetic individual and, therefore, kind. I want to caution you about the misconceptions regarding emotional intelligence. One can comprehend the essential competencies at face value, even apply them, and not be kind. Let me say that again.

People can practice emotional intelligence yet be unkind.

People can practice emotional intelligence yet be unkind.

After understanding the different types of empathy, we can recognize that some may use this skill to be manipulative. Instead of using emotional intelligence for good, they use it for selfish gain. These individuals can be charismatic, motivating, and inspiring, but ultimately out only for their own benefit. That's not practicing *high* emotional intelligence. That's perverting the skillset to be self-serving.

An example of this is the Bernie Madoff scandal. He used his cognitive empathy and relationship management skills to defraud thousands of investors out of tens of billions of dollars. He was able to speak to their pain points and was persuasive in his approach to motivate them to invest with him. He didn't care about what would happen when they lost their life savings. His social awareness was only surface-level.

You may be able to practice social awareness absent of compassionate empathy. Therefore, we need to consider what kind of empathy we practice. One can be empathetic with their head and not their heart, or be persuasive without genuinely caring.

One can argue that this is the downside of emotional intelligence. However, suppose we truly recognize high emotional intelligence and all its domains to be a skill that helps us see ourselves and others, and to create healthy relationships. In that case, we can say that someone like Bernie Madoff used aspects of emotional intelligence, but did not possess *high* emotional intelligence due to his selfishness, poor self-regulation, and ulterior motives when it came to relationship management.

Empathy is intentional and a conscious choice. Understanding the intention behind your empathy and how you engage with and motivate others is part of practicing high emotional intelligence. Are you aware of your feelings, thoughts, and behaviors? Are you regulating your emotions that can lead you to take advantage of others?

Our experiences impact and are affected by our emotions. Therefore, emotions are an essential guide to help us know how to behave towards and interact with one another and navigate the world.

In the next chapter, we will learn about how important it is to know our personal stories around emotions.

-EQ REVIEW-

- Emotions are data that help our brain recall memories and experiences.

- Emotions aren't finite but can be fleeting.

- Emotions give us the drive to act.

- Emotions help us interpret other people's feelings.

- There are three types of empathy: cognitive, emotional, and compassionate.

- Cognitive empathy is the practice of understanding what a person might be thinking.

- Emotional empathy is when you physically feel what the other person is going through.

- Compassionate empathy moves us to action in trying to help others.

- You can use emotional intelligence yet be unkind.

- Empathy is intentional and a conscious choice.

6

NARRATIVES AROUND EMOTIONS

*"Owning our story can be hard but not nearly as difficult
as spending our lives running from it."*

— *Brené Brown*

"Google."

That's the answer I received from Peter when I asked where he first learned about feelings. Let's just say I didn't have Google on my EQ BINGO card, yet, this answer intrigued me. I asked him to expound on that.

"Somewhere between when I was ideating suicide and my first same-sex relationship, which was very confusing for me to process, I realized that I needed to read up on emotions because I never gave myself a formal opportunity to learn about them."

I liked his use of the word "formal." Because, unless you go into a field like psychology, most of us don't take the time to study feelings in general or, more importantly, examine our own.

For Peter, the uncovering of emotions beyond what he already knew came at a pivotal point. While wrestling with suicidal ideation and self-identification, his search to understand feelings was essentially a search to understand himself. This is a journey that many of us experience. Suicidal ideation may not be our catalyst, but our existence is hardly void of strong emotions. On the contrary, these feelings make us feel alive and shape our lives.

During my therapy intake calls, one of the first questions I ask potential clients is, "What's going on in your life that currently has you seeking therapy?"

Hardly anyone goes to therapy because their life is perfect. There's often a tipping point where you say, "Okay, I may need some help here." I help my clients process their thoughts and feelings about current circumstances. However, the formation of these thoughts and feelings has a history. There's a story behind why you think and feel the way you do. I would be remiss if we addressed emotional intelligence without exploring our narratives around emotions.

Much of the emotional intelligence work I've seen is very present and future-focused. There are articles and training on using our EQ to bring satisfaction, joy, and success into our lives. I'm all about us living our best lives, being our happiest selves—but, more importantly, we should strive to be our healthiest selves. However, getting there may not result in immediate joy, and, sometimes, "healthy" doesn't mean "happy." For instance, some of us don't enjoy reviewing our budgets, working out, or having difficult conversations. Yet, these habits and actions improve our financial, physical, and relationship health.

In 2018, I delivered our third child. He was a whopping 10 pounds 4 ounces, and, due to his large size and fetal positioning, he ultimately weakened my pelvic floor. I would have sciatic pain and found it difficult to walk, and at times it felt as if my hip was dislocated. I didn't feel secure in my body at all. I needed physical therapy to help fix my pelvic floor and other physical issues pregnancy and labor gifted me.

One week, when walking and moving around became too painful, I requested an earlier appointment with my physical therapist. My sessions were typically an hour, but I stayed for two as my therapist tried to decrease my discomfort on this day. At the end of my session, I could barely get into my car.

With tears in my eyes, I asked my therapist how I was supposed to get home. She looked at me empathetically and said, "You will be able to make it home. Your body is doing exactly what it needs to do. Your muscles have been tightly contracted for so long that we have to relax them so they can be re-strengthened." In other words, my body had to be broken down to be built back up.

Her words were familiar. They were like the ones I tell my clients as we process their trauma—that it may feel worse before it gets better. Because you'll have to look deep into that hole you've been trying to circumvent, or that drawer or attic where you've hidden all the ugly things of your past because letting them out, you fear, will leave you undone.

For us to become self-aware, we must uncover our own stories. Very few of us take the necessary steps to discover who we are, how we got here, and how we show up in the world. The limited exploration of our emotional history hinders and impedes us from fully executing our emotional intelligence.

For us to become self-aware, we must uncover our own stories.

Family of Origin

I love a good superhero movie, especially a great origin story! They give us the backstory of how a character gained their superpowers and what made them become heroes, villains, or anti-heroes. We learn what their kryptonite or limits are, see the character's development, and learn the reasons behind their ambitions or actions. We may not be Marvel or DC comic characters, but we all have a backstory, an origin story of how we learned about feelings.

We respond and react to situations from a deeper place than we initially realize. We aren't simply responding to the words said to us by co-workers or actions we witnessed done by our friends, but from the long-term imprints of what happened to us in our younger years. As a result of our past, our responses to the current situation can be referred to as our *emotional narrative*.

We first learn about feelings through our family of origin or primary care environment. Our home life sets the stage for our emotional narratives to begin, and, from there, our education expands as we interact more with the world.

Did you grow up in a household where emotional intelligence was practiced? Were you given tools to have high-functioning relationships and a significant emotional vocabulary to express how you feel with ease? Were empathy and active listening encouraged? Was it a place where feedback was given constructively to help you grow and not kill your spirit, where everyone's emotions were validated, and everyone was held accountable for their actions?

Wait. That's not you? I bet some of you are scoffing, "Puh-leez! Feelings? We didn't talk about feelings!"

Okay, so maybe your home life wasn't like the above. Do any of these sound familiar?

"Quit your crying, or I'll give you something to cry about!"

"You are so dramatic!"

"Stop acting like a baby!"

"It's not that serious. You're fine."

Have I driven down your street yet?

Most of us weren't raised in households like the ones we watched on television. We weren't the Brady's or the Cosby's, where the parents seemed to have it all together, lovingly correcting their children and resolving problems in thirty minutes—with commercial breaks.

We may have grown up in households where it was customary to sweep things under the rug to keep up appearances. Adults didn't argue in front of the children, and experiences of discomfort, sadness, or fear were quickly shooed away. There was no need to rock the boat by being honest about how you felt. From the outside looking in, everything seemed fine. However, on the inside, folks kept tripping over a lumpy carpet that was covering all those unresolved issues.

Perhaps it was the opposite. Emotions were expressed, but they were aggressive and violent. There was shouting and cursing, hitting and throwing. The feelings were there, and like a jack-in-the-box, everyone's handle was getting cranked, but you didn't want to see what popped out. Or maybe your family life falls somewhere in between.

Take the time to reflect on whether emotions were demonstrated and talked about in healthy or unhealthy ways. When your parent or guardian was angry, did they take it out on somebody else or something else? Did they release their fury by screaming, or did they try to find relief at the bottom of a bottle? Maybe they held everything in, leaving everyone suffocating and choking on the tension in the air.

We learn specific patterns of behavior within our household. We learned that we could express our emotions and receive grace and understanding, or that we must hide our feelings because we fear the negative consequences. Some of us were provided an emotional vocabulary; others learned to be irresponsible with our emotions or express them in violent and manipulative ways.

Uncovering your emotional narrative can help you determine whether you grew up in an environment where your emotions were validated or dismissed, as well as providing insight into how you act and react to people and circumstances.

We also learn about emotions by how others describe others' behaviors to us, like a mother explaining to her children why their father yelled at them over an item being on the floor.

"Your Dad is just stressed out. You know he's had a hard day." This is what my neighbor, Angela's mother used to say to her and her siblings when their dad would come home angry.

At a young age, Angela recognized that adults' emotions were incongruent. If her father was upset with what happened at work, why didn't he say so instead of taking it out on his children? As a five-year-old, these experiences taught her that people can *choose* which emotions they want to feel and that they can also decide to put their feelings off on other people. It also taught her that we could make excuses for someone else's behavior.

"In hindsight, what my mother told us is probably what she was explaining to herself to accept his behavior or apologize for his actions," Angela, theorized thoughtfully. Isn't it interesting what emotional narratives we can create for others to help us manage our own feelings?

When we are around someone who is having a low emotional intelligence moment, we can respond by increasing our own emotional intelligence or react to their behavior based on our trauma-influenced emotional narratives. Falling back on those emotional narratives allows for acceptance of and making excuses for someone's poor behavior. At the same time, high emotional intelligence will seek to understand and possibly empathize with them, and, if needed, it will hold them accountable by bringing awareness to them. They can acknowledge the reason for the behavior without making it an excuse.

Therefore, it is vital for us to investigate emotional narratives—our own and those of others. The more we can understand what we've learned within our families and upbringing, the better we detect our default emotional reactions.

I knew a woman whose default emotions were anxiety and anger. We discovered that these would often emerge when she felt that she was in a situation where she didn't have a choice. She learned early on that, to make others happy, she had to put them before herself, and if she shared her displeasure or tried to set a boundary, it would often get ignored by her parents, or she would be persuaded to say yes.

Her "yeses" to others came at the expense of her well-being. As she explored where and why anger would bubble over, she realized that she was angry at the loss of agency. Once she was able to gain control over her story, she had more control over her emotions. She began to implement the boundaries necessary to say "yes" to herself more often, which decreased the frequency of her anger.

Social Environment

To be a good student of yourself, you must ask critical questions. What was your education around feelings? Yes, we may have watched Sesame Street and possibly had some social-emotional learning in school, but our primary lessons came from observing what we saw in our households. This teaching extended to our experiences at school, our community, and what we saw on television.

We learned what's considered acceptable by our teachers and peers within the school environment. We observed how adults communicate with one another and how they would manage the emotions and behaviors of our classmates. From a very young age, we learn how to feel, how to think about how we feel, and how to express it in our community.

Our society has taught us a lot about feelings. What do we tell young boys when they experience tender emotions like fear or sadness?

"Boys don't cry."

"Stop acting like a girl."

"You're too sensitive."

"Man up!"

"Shake it off."

Do any of these sayings sound familiar? These are the phrases that we tell boys whenever we feel discomfort over or threatened by their expression of natural feelings. Tender feelings communicate gentleness, affection, or vulnerability, as well as fear, hurt, or sadness.

We either rush them through their feelings or shame them for having them. We limit their range of emotional expression and vocabulary by doing so. This causes them to take longer to express feelings, or when they're expressed, these feelings can be quick-tempered, apathetic, or indifferent. Either way, it's unhealthy and unproductive.

It's okay for men to be angry, but, as we learned earlier, anger can sometimes be a secondary emotion. What these men may be feeling is sadness, grief, or fear. In our culture, it's neither okay nor "manly" to be tender. So, what happens? We get men who feel deep emotions but are unsure of how to express them because they've never been given permission to do so or learned how. They've been taught that some feelings aren't safe to emote. These innocent boys grow up to become men that can only convey restricted emotions.

We are left with what is called toxic masculinity. Our culture has typecast "manliness" and put pressure on men to behave in a certain way that negatively affects them—and us all. During crises like the recent pandemic that bring about many difficult emotions, being empathetic is essential. Whether it's in your role as a parent, partner, or president, being able to show compassion and be emotionally agile can help you lead well in and out of the home.

However, many men have found it challenging to extend empathy and express their anxieties or concerns for fear of appearing weak. They are uncertain, grieving, and want gentleness, but we've left them with few resources and tools. So, instead of the tenderness that needs to be seen, felt, and supported, we get aloofness or anger.

I have a childhood classmate who tragically lost her son. Sadly, she shared that there wasn't one card written or signed by a man out of all the cards her family received. During the funeral, where hundreds came to mourn, only a handful of men approached her while making eye contact or with a hug. Not one father of her son's friends came to their home, only the women. There was only one father whose son wasn't even close to hers who wept at her doorstep.

She holds the image of him weeping in her mind because it was a powerful and honorable gift. It was a display of his humanity grieving for their loss, and that's what they needed from their community, especially from the men. Even within her grief group, there were only two men. What example does this set for our boys? That they only see women nurturing and being nurtured in bereavement.

There are few safe spaces for boys to express themselves fully. Unfortunately, they continue to face this challenge as adults. Many of the men I interviewed shared that it's easier for them to talk to women. "Women like to talk. Women listen." Regardless of sexual orientation, women are a form of an emotional outlet for these men. For some, this outlet still doesn't provide complete safety to be tender; rather, it allows them the exercise of sharing their thoughts that respond to women's feelings but not necessarily addressing their own.

Similar messaging is given to young girls that limit the healthy expression of their feelings.

"You're so emotional."

"You should smile more."

"Don't be a baby."

"You're so bossy."

"Be nice."

There are expectations of what little girls should look and act like. She can't be too vocal, too sad, or too "boyish." If she takes a leadership role, she's deemed bossy. As she grows into an articulate and assertive woman, she's labeled angry or called out of her name. If she shows vulnerability where tears may flow, she's viewed as weak and overly emotional—and yet, if she's not "soft" enough, her femininity comes into question.

The external narrative that women receive is that their feelings need to bring comfort to others. They can't be "overly emotional" or too stoic. Their disposition needs to be disarming. They are also told to "Calm down!" and that it must be "that time of the month" when they express their emotions. Although women are given more permission to express their feelings publicly, these feelings are still scrutinized. They need to be pleasant and non-threatening. Emotional frustration is not allowed.

Our societal emotional narratives blur our vision. Women in politics seem to be measured more by their personality and likeability than their experience or competency. They must be careful of how they express their emotions. They have to be nice, but not too nice. They try to appease all sexes. If they show that they are "tough" like the guys, it's a turnoff. They are viewed as weak or infantilized if they show too much femininity.

The same emotions attributed to men as strengths are those women are punished for. We've witnessed this often in professional sports. A man's anger is described as passionate, while a woman's anger is reported as unhinged.

What society has prescribed as signs of weakness in men isn't inherently viewed as a power source for women. Ironically, tender emotions are equally ridiculed and dismissed by men and women, and then we wonder why kindness, compassion, and gentleness are anemic in our homes, schools, workplaces, and communities.

Society has done a successful job of telling all of us how we should act and feel. We've never read a script, yet we know how to play our parts well. Those who choose to adlib are punished. There's an expected performance that some may find easier to conform to than others. How often are we exerting energy to perform as "boys should" or as "girls should," knowing that it wasn't always how we wanted to express ourselves?

EQ Reflection: What messages were you given as a child about feelings? Were they good messages? How did they shape your beliefs regarding how you show up in the world and what you expect from others? Can you see how these narratives around emotions have shaped you?

Our culture has erected rigid boundaries that define masculinity and femininity, falsely characterizing emotions, manipulating us to keep up with gender roles that don't benefit us when we want to be vulnerable and unpack and cope with what is affecting us. These inflexible roles have perpetuated homophobia, domination, exclusion, and "imposter syndrome" and have negatively impacted our mental health.

These feelings that we have come from somewhere. With all its idiosyncrasies, habits, and behaviors, your identity combines your lived experiences and learning. They become the stories that unfold as we engage with our world.

I don't know if your emotional narratives are tragedies, dark comedies, or ones of survival. Take heart. I have good news. Your history cannot be re-written, but your present and future stories can be developed into a narrative that casts you as a protagonist whose elevated emotional intelligence will benefit you.

-EQ REVIEW-

- Our responses to current situations that are influenced by our pasts can be referred to as our emotional narrative.

- For us to become more self-aware, we must uncover our own stories.

- Uncovering your emotional narrative can help you determine whether you grew up in an environment where your emotions were validated or dismissed.

- We all have stories involving how we learned about feelings.

- We learn about feelings from our family of origin, home life, school, and society.

- Emotionally intelligent homes are empathetic. Members actively listen. Feedback is given constructively, and emotions are validated and held accountable.

- There are few safe spaces for boys to express themselves fully.

- The external narrative that women receive is that their feelings need to bring comfort to others.

- The same emotions attributed to men as strengths are those women are punished for.

- Your future narratives can change.

7

BARRIERS TO EMOTIONAL INTELLIGENCE

"The single biggest problem in communication is the illusion that it has taken place."

— *George Bernard Shaw*

When I was growing up, we used to play a game called "Telephone." It's a cooperative game that works best in a large group. The premise was that you would say a word or a phrase to the first person, and they would then whisper the word or phrase to the person next to them. Each player would do this until it got to the last player. Then, they would say aloud what they heard so everyone could hear how much the word or phrase had changed from the first whisper.

What started as "The best chips are chocolate ones," somehow turns into "We sent ships with ice cream cones."

But a message doesn't need to go around a circle to get lost in translation: the message can change just between two people. This is because different barriers impact how we communicate with and interpret emotions in others. Acknowledging these barriers can help us improve our emotional intelligence. We must first identify our barriers and understand or at least be aware of the possible barriers others have. By doing so, we can determine which domain of emotional intelligence we must increase.

Acknowledge barriers in self – **Self-Awareness**

Manage the emotions that surface as you recognize your barriers – **Self-Management**

Acknowledge barriers in others – **Social Awareness**

Improve communication skills with others by actively listening – **Relationship Management**

Family of Origin

In the previous chapter, you learned how your family of origin set the stage for your emotional narratives. Your upbringing can also create barriers that limit your ability to perceive emotions within yourself and others. Studies have shown that if you grew up in a household where there was addiction, neglect, or abuse, it is more difficult for you to read the positive or neutral facial expressions of others.

This can lead to interpreting neutrality as negative and believing that someone is upset when they're not. Because of the unpredictability of your home, you were often on guard and looking to determine whether it was safe. Your self-talk may have been, "Is Daddy happy drunk or angry drunk?"

These early childhood experiences can leave you misinterpreting someone's emotions, leading you to make assumptions. You've heard what they say about when you assume: you make an A-S-S out of U and ME, and I don't think any of us want to be one. These assumptions can decrease both your social awareness and your ability to healthily manage relationships.

EQ-Tip

To lower EQ barriers, increase your active listening skills and become more curious. Asking clarifying questions like, "I know that you said you were pleased with this decision, but I can't tell from your facial expression. Can you tell me what you're feeling?"

This allows the other person to confirm or clarify their thoughts and feelings. You don't want to infer. Yes, it may seem like additional work, but if you have a history of misreading people, it can save you a lot of headaches in the long run. I genuinely feel sorry for those poor souls who must deal with people misinterpreting their neutral affect daily, when their resting face unintentionally appears angry, annoyed, or irritated.

Also, coming from a home that devalues emotions or causes discomfort when displaying tender feelings can cause a barrier. We end up trying to avoid these feelings within ourselves or when they're expressed by others. We may also feel a sense of shame. If this response to emotions is learned during your upbringing, you will have to learn how to build your emotional tolerance. You may have learned to rush through feelings or try to rush others through feelings that make you uncomfortable.

EQ-Tip

Practicing self-awareness and self-management will help you in this area. An exercise you can do is what is called *emotional exposure therapy*. What you would do is watch a television show or a movie, where you can learn to gradually sit with your feelings to begin getting familiar and more comfortable with them.

Watching a show like *This is Us* or movies like *Crash* or *Dead Poets Society* can bring a lot of emotions to the surface. Acknowledge the sadness or other emotions of sensitivity within yourself to build tolerance and resilience.

Life Circumstances

As life evolves, so does our emotional intelligence. When I became a mother with a newborn who wouldn't sleep, my EQ decreased with each sleepless night. Brain cells seemed to float out of my ears and pop out of existence like bubbles blown from a wand.

"You told me this already," my husband would say, as I didn't realize I was repeating myself. Then, the next moment, I'd be in the middle of a sentence and completely forget what I was saying. Hence the cycle of repetitive storytelling.

With the short-term memory loss, I became curt and impatient. Anger readily took over, and the tact I was known for showed up less and less. That poor man had to deal with me snapping on him from the way he fastened diapers to how loudly I thought he breathed. Imagine being someone who teaches and understands the importance of emotional intelligence becoming deficient in its practice!

I know that some people can still be functional while sleep-deprived. I'm not one of them. I value rest so much that naps are a staple in my self-care toolbox. So, it came as no surprise that, as my infant's sleep didn't improve but became worse, postpartum depression set in. Of course, I understood my circumstances. I have and did give myself grace, but I'm highlighting that fatigue and stress can wear you out, making it challenging to show up for yourself and others well.

EQ-Tip

Recognize what season of life you are in. Are you a new parent? Have you recently been promoted? Are you in the process of a separation? These situations not only impact your mental health, but they can also impact your emotional intelligence. Own that you are in an adjusting period and may need to set firmer boundaries around your time and with whom you speak. Even when stressed, you can still implement EQ strategies. You may be struggling to self-manage, but you can still practice self-awareness and relationship management while articulating where you are. Saying, "Hey, I'm stressed, I don't think I can be my best self for you right now," is still using your emotional intelligence. This allows the other person to better manage their expectations.

Trauma

Trauma is an event or a series of events that an individual can experience that can adversely affect their mental, physical, social, emotional, and spiritual well-being and cause a significant barrier to practicing emotional intelligence.

It isn't easy to self-regulate when our amygdala (our feeling brain) is activated, and we shift into survival mode. Depending on the trauma, it can make us wary and distrustful of others and ourselves.

For those who have experienced sexual trauma, being violated in this way can cause you to distrust your feelings or ignore them altogether.

There was a young woman who had been sexually assaulted several times in her youth. After she had attended a professional event, one of her male colleagues offered her a ride back to her hotel. Since she was from out of town, she accepted his offer.

When they arrived at the hotel, he suggested that he walk in with her. "It's late, I don't know if it's safe for you to walk in alone."

At this moment, she felt unsettled, but didn't decline the invitation as his reasoning made sense. Once inside the hotel lobby, he proposed to walk her up to her room for "safety reasons."

A voice inside of her told her "no" but it was hard to trust her discernment, as well as to dismiss the well-thought-out argument this colleague was presenting. Unfortunately, the colleague took advantage of her trust and assaulted her.

Trauma can make emotions tricky. In my work with survivors of sexual assault and abuse, I have found that they can be overwhelmed by their feelings, yet they also disregard or invalidate their feelings or needs and unintentionally mistreat themselves similarly to their abusers who ignored their boundaries and manipulated their emotions. It isn't uncommon for adults who were emotionally abused in childhood to display insecurity in problem-solving and decision-making and feel easily offended or humiliated.

Emotional Barriers

ANGER

When all we see is red, we can't see anything else. When anger gets the best of us and we behave poorly, we tend to say, "I blacked out." Again, it signifies a limited perspective. Anger is detrimental to our communication because we are less logical. Our amygdala is arrested, and it seems like our prefrontal cortex is a long way away.

Our anger affects how our brain processes information. We are filtering the information through a warped lens. We begin to read into what another person is saying or doing. Anger makes it challenging to listen actively, which doesn't help us with managing conflict or resolving problems.

When I conduct training programs on using emotional intelligence when negotiating, I teach how anger can kill a deal. Yes, it may make us feel powerful and in control, but if the anger is left unchecked, we can be out of control.

Juan, was a general contractor who was trying to secure a loan with a bank. He was getting frustrated with their process and began to demand they expedite it. He caught wind that they had provided a loan for another general contractor who he had previously done some work for. He began to speak about this other contractor in disparaging ways to one of the bankers. Juan's anger and poor character cost him the loan as the bankers recognized that he wouldn't be a cooperative customer.

Being angry can negatively impact relationships by escalating conflict and decreasing cooperation. It also makes you less accurate in recalling your interests (low self-awareness) and assessing the other party's interests (low social awareness and relationship management). The person on the receiving end may feel frightened, defensive, or hurt by your anger, which ruins the chances of a positive and productive negotiation. Remember, no one wants to work with a hothead.

EQ-Tip

Check yourself! Remove yourself from an emotionally charged situation so you can cool off. Taking a moment to walk away and regulate your emotions will allow you to calm down your amygdala and start activating the boss of your brain. Hello Charlie.

Remember: while you're angry, you'll have trouble processing what is going on. Give yourself a chance to calm down to get a clearer picture. You'll find that taking a needed break will help to improve your communication and decision-making.

ANXIETY

Anxiety or fear can cause us to avoid having difficult conversations. These could be requesting constructive feedback, disciplining your child, or discussing serious topics like racism. It's said that the acronym for fear is False Evidence Appearing Real, and for the most part, I would agree. Fear causes us to think about the worst-case scenario. Now, granted, there are some legitimate fears, like when a wild animal is chasing you or you're not able to afford your high medical bills, but, often, the things we fear are not life-threatening. However, if we don't pull on that leash, our anxious thoughts can have us quickly spiraling down a rabbit hole or limit us from achieving what we really want.

Anxiety will have you believe that people-pleasing and being conflict-avoidant will garner healthy relationships. False. This will only create imbalanced and disingenuous relationships. Your fear will lead you to do things out of compulsion and not by choice.

EQ-Tip

Practice some relaxation exercises. After you've relaxed, ask yourself if there's evidence to back up your fear. Does your boss really hate you? Is your boyfriend going to break up with you? If so, what proof do you have of this? Learning to slow yourself down with breathing techniques can allow you to assess the situation more accurately.

APATHY

Although apathy isn't a heightened expression of emotion, it can still cause problems within relationships. Apathy is a lack of interest in or concern about matters that should interest you. It's an "I don't care" attitude that can cause conflict with others. Because apathy can come across as negative, it can provoke a strong response from others.

They may choose not to engage with you if they feel you are disinterested or unmotivated. This behavior can decrease morale and discourage others. This is the person you don't want to work with within a group project because they either put in little effort or are pessimistic and shoot down every idea without offering a solution.

EQ-Tip

There can be several reasons behind your apathy. Take the time to practice self-awareness so you can examine your feelings and ask yourself the critical questions to determine why you're disengaged. Apathy is a typical response to major stress. It can also be a symptom of burnout.

If you recognize that apathy has become more commonplace, it may be helpful to seek counseling. You want to make sure you address the disinterest early on before it leads to more severe symptoms of depression if sustained too long.

PRIDE

We've all met someone who can easily see the speck in someone else's eye but fails to see the log in their own. This self-absorption and pride can be another barrier. Speaking with a "know-it-all" isn't fun. It's a struggle to have a healthy conversation with someone who needs to be right all the time or have the last word. Everything you say seems to be ignored. The other person dismisses what you say and quickly brings the conversation back to them. Because they can't see past their own nose, they aren't listening to you, nor do they care to acknowledge your thoughts and feelings. To them, you are more of an audience member than an active participant.

When only listening to one voice—their own—there isn't room for collaboration or presenting the best solutions. Whether in the boardroom or the bedroom, taking note of others' contributions to the conversation and validating their thoughts and feelings fosters trust and respect.

Pride can get in the way of reconciliation. It can be infuriating when someone has caused harm, but their pride doesn't allow them to take ownership of their wrongdoing. They don't manage relationships well because they don't manage themselves well.

When we struggle with pride, we can't practice social awareness and empathize with others because we aren't reading their emotions. This is because we're focused on *who?* Ourselves. I know this probably isn't you, but if it is, read the next EQ-Tip.

EQ-Tip

Practice active listening techniques and slow down to let the other person speak. Repeat back what you heard them say, for example: "What I'm hearing you say is. . ." or "It sounds like you enjoyed your family trip." Pause to self-reflect if the conversation is bringing up any emotional insecurities. Emotionally intelligent conversations allow room for acceptance of imperfections in others and yourself. Recognize when you are monopolizing the conversation, deflecting, or assuming a sense of superiority while speaking.

Accepting your mistakes or highlighting someone else's ideas is not a sign of weakness. On the contrary, people will be more open to speaking with you because you've demonstrated humility. Trust me, your partners, children, friends, and colleagues will appreciate this behavior change.

NEURODIVERGENCE

Chris keeps saying he needs to schedule a call with you, but he never does. Not because he doesn't want to; he simply forgets. Why does Angela keep forgetting your name, and constantly interrupts you when you are speaking.

For my readers who have ADHD, you know where I'm going with this. It's not that you mean to leave people hanging, but there's something to the "out of sight, out of mind" concept that holds some truth. It doesn't mean that you don't care; it's just one of the ways the ADHD brain works.

Neurodivergent means "to have differing mental or neurological function from what is considered typical." It is frequently used with reference to Autism Spectrum Disorder, ADHD, dyspraxia, and dyslexia all fall within the spectrum of "neurodiversity," or those who are not neurotypical.

ADHD and other forms of neurodivergence entail symptoms that can negatively impact emotional clarity. In general, people with ADHD tend to have difficulty with social skills because there's a lower ability to recognize emotions in others, impulsivity, and they feel emotions intensely. If your ADHD co-occurs with anxiety, it can increase your challenges with self-regulation.

DISABILITIES

Several years ago, one of our church members experienced a stroke. It limited his ability to communicate verbally and to visually express his emotions. Speaking with him required additional patience and creativity in communication. There was more of a need to ask clarifying questions because you literally couldn't take what he said at face value. A stroke or accident can cause a physical barrier to communication.

Illnesses like dementia and Alzheimer's can also cause challenges. If the relationship is one of familiarity, it can be difficult for both parties. Feelings of grief may become present because what used to come with ease has become difficult. We must be careful with this grief. It can add an additional barrier to communication.

If self-management isn't practiced, the grief can cause us to become less patient, causing us to rush the interaction, become dismissive, or project our feelings onto the other person. Our frustration and sadness are natural responses to this change but are not excuses to treat the other person poorly.

Someone who has a hearing loss or an auditory processing disorder can miss important pieces of information, have difficulty following complex directions, or won't be able to hear the tone of someone's voice. When someone starts losing their hearing, they may not notice it at first, but eventually, it hinders the flow of communication. They don't hear or mishear details completely, preventing them from being in tune without knowing it. For a deaf person, their primary form of communication may be through sign language. This can limit how they engage with others. However, they may be better at reading non-verbal cues.

These hiccups in communication can be frustrating on both ends. We want to engage but can find ourselves exhausted or annoyed when repeating ourselves. Or, if we are the ones losing our sense of hearing, we can become flustered or embarrassed when we begin to realize that our hearing changes are causing a change in our relationships.

A congenital disability like hearing loss or visual impairment can be a challenge in practicing our emotional intelligence. A person who is blind or visually impaired may not be able to read body language or see facial expressions fully, or at all. However, they can verbally communicate and be more sensitive to tone.

The loss of hearing or sight doesn't necessarily mean that those with the disability will be deficient in their emotional intelligence; it simply means that, to navigate the world, they must learn how to communicate differently to help them in their social awareness and relationship management.

On the other hand, those without these disabilities tend to be challenged when engaging with individuals with disabilities. Sometimes, awareness of a disability can stir up emotions of confusion or discomfort. If we aren't practicing self-awareness and self-management, we can behave and respond in a manner that can cause those individuals to feel othered due to our ableist way of thinking. Ableism is discrimination and social prejudice against people with disabilities based on the belief that typical abilities are superior. This leads us to our next barrier. Bias.

BIAS

In the summer of 2001, I studied abroad in São Paulo, Brazil. I didn't speak a lick of Portuguese and barely knew any Spanish, but there I was, in a different country, staying with a host mother who spoke and understood very little English. To communicate effectively, as best as we could, we had to listen intently to one another, use objects when necessary, or make exaggerated facial expressions to convey our messages.

In the beginning, language was a barrier, but it didn't diminish our ability to communicate. As time went on, my Portuguese improved, which brought my host mother and me closer. We enjoyed long and deep conversations, her with her broken English and me with my broken Portuguese. It was one of the best times of my life.

The same couldn't be said for Cindy, one of my classmates who attended with me. She told me how she didn't connect with her host family at all. Unfortunately, she let the language barrier become a ten foot wall between her and them.

One day I went to visit Cindy and witnessed how she would shut herself away in her room and wouldn't speak to anyone. Her Brazilian family told me how they were so sad because they wanted her to feel at home, but she wouldn't communicate with them.

I was confused so I asked her what the reason for her behavior was.

"I feel stupid speaking Portuguese. I wished they'd speak English."

I looked at her incredulously and said, "Girl, we're in *Brazil*!"

The more time we spent together, I realized that it wasn't only the culture shock that Cindy was experiencing but also a lack of cultural awareness. As a White woman in her early twenties from the Midwest, she was used to the comfort of being part of the majority culture. You can say that being "different" felt different. Yes, I could empathize with her anxiety and feeling homesick. However, her attitude and remarks were evidence of something else. As time went on, my new thought was, "Your bias is showing!"

It wasn't just hers; I observed similar behavior from several of the White American students in our group.

"I don't know why everyone is late here."

"This wouldn't be acceptable in America."

"There's so much crime and poor people here."

Where curiosity about a new culture could have opened the door to understanding, I witnessed judgment. There's a way that you can ask "why" that sparks interest or promotes critique.

Along with myself, the two other students of color, one from Ecuador and the other a Black American, would watch as our Brazilian professor did her best to respond to these remarks with civility, but there were moments where she was clearly exasperated and would simply respond, "This is Brazil, not the U.S."

Biases, along with other forms of discrimination, don't cultivate healthy and safe interactions. When we know that someone is looking at us from a biased viewpoint, our words, expressions, and the way we look are filtered through a lens that obscures their vision. Therefore, when we think about the four domains of emotional intelligence, they don't fire on all cylinders when our biases are at play.

Bias stems from the human brain's tendency to categorize new people and new information. Our brains are actively trying to make the world make sense to us. However, the way our brain processes information is not without influence. Our culture and experiences have an effect on it.

Therefore, if our culture is riddled with systems of inequity, the prevalent inclination for or against something or someone is learned. This learning can create erroneous beliefs about others, which stifles healthy human relationships and connections.

It is this barrier erected as a result of inequity that we will unpack together. Now that we've understood emotional intelligence in black and white, let's add some color.

-EQ REVIEW-

- Our family of origin and our upbringing can create barriers that limit our ability to perceive emotions within ourselves and others.

- Emotional intelligence can evolve over time due to life circumstances.

- Trauma can construct a significant barrier to practicing emotional intelligence. Depending on the trauma, it can make us wary and distrustful.

- Some emotional barriers to emotional intelligence include anger, anxiety, apathy, and pride.

- Neurodivergence, such as ADHD, can negatively impact emotional clarity.

- Disabilities such as hearing loss and vision impairment can challenge our emotional intelligence.

- There are those without disabilities who may have difficulty engaging with those with disabilities because they haven't practiced self-awareness and self-management. Their ableism gets in the way of their relationship management.

- Biases, along with other forms of discrimination, don't allow for the cultivation of healthy and safe interactions.

PART TWO:

EMOTIONAL INTELLIGENCE IN COLOR

***

Emotional intelligence is a nuanced skill that is influenced in its practice by a variety of things, including systems of oppression and inequity. If we are truly honest with ourselves, what aspects of our lives have not been impacted by them? Racism, sexism, ableism—you choose an -ism, one or more have affected our personal lives.

While emotional intelligence is a skill set that is gaining appreciation in the workplace, we are not all using it in the same way. Those of us who have been marginalized or underrepresented use the four domains quite differently. I wanted you to have a basic understanding of this skill so you could better understand the discussion about what it looks like in practice by Black individuals and those from other systemically marginalized groups when they navigate predominantly White, male, and heterosexual spaces.

8

RACIAL TRAUMA

"Prejudice is a burden that confuses the past, threatens the future, and renders the present inaccessible."

– Maya Angelou

Can you remember a particular time when you were stressed? You were so overwhelmed and didn't know what to do. Maybe it caused you to have difficulty sleeping. Whatever the issue was, you couldn't wait for it to be over.

We've all experienced stress, and it sucks. However, stress isn't always bad. There are times when stress can be motivating and give us the push that we need to accomplish something, like tackling an approaching deadline. We can also experience positive stress when we feel excited about a date or competing in a game. This is called eustress.

On the flip side, stress can become debilitating. I think of those who suffer from test or performance anxiety or experience obsessive-compulsive disorder (OCD). The stress doesn't spur them on but stops them dead in their tracks.

When we are stressed, our bodies release the hormone cortisol. It's our body's natural survival response to move us to action. For example, when avoiding an accident, or completing a difficult task, the right amount of stress can increase alertness and performance. However, our bodies aren't meant to stay in this state of hypervigilance for an extended period.

An overabundance of cortisol has adverse effects on our overall health. Bad stress causes irritability, difficulty concentrating, increased inflammation, high blood pressure, diabetes, decreased immunity and hormone production, hair loss, depression, and anxiety, just to name a few.

As a clinician, I am aware of the mental health crisis caused by the stress stemming from the Covid-19 pandemic. We have been forever changed. We are not the same people we were back in March of 2020. Equally, as a Black woman living in the United States, I'm profoundly aware of the mental health crisis that has been brought on by racism. Even if we weren't dealing with a pandemic, racism brings its own measure of stress and trauma.

We defined trauma in the last chapter as an event or a series of events that an individual can experience that can adversely affect their mental, physical, social, emotional, and spiritual well-being. There are four forms:

Acute Trauma results from exposure to a single overwhelming traumatic event or experience.

Chronic Trauma may include one or multiple forms of trauma that repeatedly occur(s) over an extended period.

Complex Trauma is exposure to numerous traumatic events or experiences in early childhood and its immediate adverse effects.

Historical Trauma is cumulative mass group exposure to adverse experiences across generations.

PTSD or Post Traumatic Stress Disorder can occur after a person has experienced or witnessed a traumatic event. For Black individuals, the P in PTSD stands for past, present, and persistent. Due to its pervasive nature, there's this nuance of learning how to heal yourself while you are consistently being harmed. There's nothing "post" about it. Whether it's through experiencing microaggressions or being traumatized by what they see and read in the news, Black individuals and others who are excluded because of their ethnicity live with the daily stress and trauma of racism.

Now, let's define racism.

Racism is prejudice against, discrimination towards, or antagonism by an individual, community, or institution aimed at a person or people based on their belonging to a particular racial or ethnic group.

Racism comes in three forms:

- Systemic
- Interpersonal
- Internalized

Systemic racism occurs when ideologies, institutions, and policies create racial and ethnic inequality. Historical examples of systemic or structural racism include removing American-Indian children from their families throughout the nineteenth century and the forcible internment of Japanese Americans in concentration camps during World War II.

Let's not forget the 250 years of slavery in the United States, followed by 100 years of Jim Crow laws deliberately designed to restrict the rights of Black Americans. Systemic racism is so embedded in systems that it often is assumed to reflect the natural, inevitable order of things.

The discriminatory laws created by systemic racism exemplify how systems and structures built upon greed and hatred are fueled by thinking that typifies low emotional intelligence. These laws are not to serve all but to selfishly serve a selected group.

Social awareness and relationship management are not at play within these systems because there's a lack of empathy and intentional disregard for the well-being and experience of others. There's also a lack of self-awareness and self-management. These practices would ordinarily regulate feelings of fear and inadequacy related to engaging with other races and ethnicities, but their absence leads one to create a system of superiority and othering.

Internalized racism occurs when one accepts negative stereotypes and social beliefs about one's racial group.

When the movie Black Panther came out, I was so excited! I told you that I love a good superhero movie. I was fascinated with everything about this film. I was too eager to watch when I discovered a behind-the-scenes video with director Ryan Coogler breaking down one of the fight scenes.

Before the "Notes on a Scene" episode, I had never heard Ryan speak, so imagine my surprise when within the first 45 seconds of the nine-and-a-half-minute video, all I could think was, "I didn't know he talked like that."

I was dismayed as I listened to his tone and use of African American Vernacular English (AAVE). However, by the second-minute mark, I exclaimed that this man was a genius! Then, I had to sit with the awareness of my thoughts and feelings. I was disheartened and embarrassed that I had judged this brilliant Black man by how he spoke.

I had internalized the racist idea that intelligence had a sound, and it didn't come in AAVE's cadence, tone, and language. My heart hurt as I acknowledged how much racism has impacted even how Black people see each other—believing that White is right and that Black is wack.

Another example is the belief that having a darker complexion is less attractive, therefore causing one to favor lighter skin tones. This is called *colorism*.

This form of prejudice within the same ethnic or racial group is perpetuated within society, like that of India, where the darker you are, the lower you are in the caste system. The lighter you are in China, the more noble you are considered. Within the United States, during the time of slavery, the African Americans who were darker worked in the fields while those with lighter skin were often given more domestic tasks, hence the terms "field negro" and "house negro."

In the famous 1940s doll experiment by Kenneth and Mamie Clark, Black children were handed four dolls: two had dark skin, and two had light skin. The results showed that the majority of Black children preferred the White dolls. When asked about characteristics, like "good" or "bad," the negative characteristics would be attributed to the Black dolls.

Can I let you in on a little secret? This test has been recreated, and not much has changed in over seventy years. When given a choice, Black children will prefer to play with the White doll and treat it better than the Black one. What does that mean? There is still anti-Black bias even as we have become a more integrated society.

Lastly, there's **interpersonal racism**, which involves two or more people and can manifest as bigotry, bias, prejudice, or microaggressions. Sometimes, these instances of interpersonal racism are violent and have long-term impacts on their respective communities, or even nationwide.

One of the worst instances of violent interpersonal racism in our nation's history was the 1921 Tulsa Race Massacre. From May 31 to June 1, 1921, a White mob destroyed what was referred to as "Black Wall Street." It was a thriving African American community in Tulsa's Greenwood neighborhood. 300 African Americans were killed, and 10,000 were displaced.

There have been many blatant incidents of interpersonal racism throughout American history, including the 1873 Colfax Massacre, the 1908 Springfield Race Riot, and the 1950s and 1960s Civil Rights Era, just to name a few.

However, more frequently, interpersonal racism happens on a "smaller" scale, during daily interactions. These instances often involve microaggressions. We will discuss microaggressions more in Chapter 10.

Now that we have defined trauma and understand the different forms of racism, by putting the two together, we get racial trauma, or race-based stress. This trauma refers to the mental and emotional injury caused by encounters with racial bias, ethnic discrimination, racism, and hate crimes.

The viewing of videos of police killings of Black people, the increased violence against Asian women, and the high rates of societal homicide and suicide of Native American children causes traumatic stress reactions in the people who view or are witness to them. This is called vicarious or secondary trauma.

As we understand the link between trauma and stress, if someone experiences chronic and historical trauma, the cortisol level within their body remains elevated for extended periods. This sustained overabundance of cortisol can change one's gene expression, and these changes can be passed down from one generation to the next.

Those who are descendants of chattel slavery in the United States and other countries have experienced historical trauma. In some cases, they've experienced all four types. This historical experience serves as a source of traumatic stress for Black people today. We now have a group of people whose genetic makeup has been changed by this trauma's hereditary nature, which makes them more susceptible to the health risks we discussed earlier.

Many of us never fully understood the hereditary nature of race-based trauma. We are unaware of how it affects our peers. We assume that one must live through that trauma—for example, the trauma of enslavement—to feel its effects, but the transgenerational impact is profound. We must be thoughtful of the lineage of those who have gone through this trauma to better understand their story and their conscious and subconscious predispositions when we engage with them, whether in the workplace or in our personal lives.

WEATHERING

Unfortunately, microaggressions are commonplace and add to the daily emotional tax that many historically marginalized and under-represented people face. This taxation arises from being made to feel different from your peers because of your gender, race, and ethnicity. It brings along its own level of fear of being stereotyped or receiving unfair treatment. This leaves one feeling othered or alienated from their peers.

Being told to ignore microaggressions still puts the burden on those who experience them to discern whether the bigotry they face is real or only perceived, or whether it's intentional or unintentional, and then to ignore their natural emotional response to being treated in such a way. The term *weathering* refers to how the constant stress of racism can lead to adverse health outcomes for racially marginalized people.

"I started losing my hair and having panic attacks," one woman told me as she explained why she left her six-figure corporate position.

Her work environment was toxic; she experienced both racial discrimination and sexual harassment. The human resources department ignored her pleas and left her questioning her sanity. As her relationships also began to deteriorate, she decided to quit her job. "The job was breaking me down, and I had to leave if I wanted to save my life."

The fear of losing her life is a legitimate fear. Racial discrimination is a social issue *and* a public health issue. The wear and tear of weathering causes premature aging, along with other physiological and biological effects. A 2018 study found that Black adults between the ages of 48 and 60 had a biological age that was 2.6 years *older* than their chronological age.

In other words, Black adults "weathered 6.1 years faster" than White adults.

The average biological age among White adults was 3.5 years *younger* than their chronological age. In other words, Black adults "weathered 6.1 years faster" than White adults.

The weathering isn't only physiological; it's psychological. My client's boss called on him twice during a Zoom meeting. "Tony, are you with us? You haven't said anything."

My client wasn't sure if his new boss was trying to be inclusive or if she was trying to throw him under the bus. She seemed nice, but my client didn't know her well enough to decipher her actions. I recall him saying, "Just the exercise of figuring out if this was a racial aggression or if it was just a poor leadership style is exhausting. You never know with White people."

It is draining to have to process most experiences this way. Some might say that it's an unnecessary process. To suggest this is to ignore the historical and personal experiences of those who've been marginalized on account of their race.

You might be thinking, *But, Farah, not all White people. . .* To that, I will leave what boxer and activist Muhammad Ali said in his 1971 interview in *Parkinson*. He stated:

> "There are many White people who mean right and in their hearts wanna do right. If 10,000 snakes were coming down that aisle now, and I had a door that I could shut, and in that 10,000, 1,000 meant right, 1,000 rattlesnakes didn't want to bite me, I *knew* they were good. . . Should I let all these rattlesnakes come down, hoping that

that thousand get together and form a shield? Or should I just close the door and stay safe?"

Having to process experiences by asking yourself questions like, "Was that racist?" is tiring. There's the desire to give the person the benefit of the doubt in the hope that the unsettling feeling you're experiencing is inaccurate and that you're simply misinterpreting the situation.

This mental exercise of determining whether something or someone had racist intent and what and who is safe impacts our well-being and how we practice emotional intelligence. For example, when someone engages with you in a racially insensitive or ambiguously offensive way, there's often the need to recognize the offender's feelings and place them above your own.

Racial trauma can be experienced anywhere and at any time. At work, at school, running through a neighborhood, playing outside, while shopping, bird watching, or going to Starbucks. However, racial trauma expert and therapist Ashley McGirt, LICSW, states that "[r]acial trauma at work is especially insidious. It can be the worst kind of racial trauma as we often spend more time at work than we do with our own families." We can also say this about those who experience racial trauma in the classroom, as our children spend more time at school than they do at home.

Our brain experiences the workplace and educational institutions first and foremost as a social system. As human beings, we are created for community. During primitive times, when we had to protect ourselves from wildlife, it was best to stay with the group for our survival.

We no longer have to fight off animals in the wild, but we still have this natural desire to be connected. To belong. To be a part of something. When we experience microaggressions and other actions that can cause us to feel othered, our brains process these rejections as physical pain.

Trauma soils so many facets of our lives, from how we express our emotions and our identity to how we relate to one another. Racism and other forms of discrimination and inequity impact how we choose to navigate stressful situations with regard to our emotions.

It teaches us how we should adjust our behavior to assimilate and minimize the potential harm endured from hate and bigotry. When we experience trauma and stress, we learn survival skills to keep us safe from a world that harms us.

One particular survival skill is code-switching—though, is it really a *survival skill*, or is it something else? Let's find out together.

-EQ REVIEW-

- Positive stress is called eustress.

- When we are stressed, our bodies release the hormone cortisol.

- Our bodies aren't meant to stay in a state of hypervigilance for an extended period due to cortisol's adverse effects on our overall health.

- There are four types of trauma: acute, chronic, complex, and historical.

  o **Acute Trauma** results from exposure to a single overwhelming event traumatic or experience.

  o **Chronic Trauma** includes one or multiple forms of trauma that repeatedly occur over an extended period.

  o **Complex Trauma** is exposure to multiple traumatic events or experiences in early childhood and its immediate adverse effects.

  o **Historical Trauma** is cumulative mass group exposure to adverse experiences across generations.

- Racism comes in three forms:

  o **Systemic** - when ideologies, institutions, practices, and policies operate to produce racial and ethnic inequality.

  o **Interpersonal** - involves two or more people. It can manifest in the form of bigotry, bias, prejudice, and microaggressions.

  o **Internalized** - the acceptance of negative stereotypes and social beliefs about one's own racial group.

    ▪ *Colorism* - prejudice or discrimination against individuals with a dark skin tone, typically among people of the same ethnic or racial group.

- Racial trauma refers to the mental and emotional injury caused by encounters with racial bias, ethnic discrimination, racism, and hate crimes.

- Our brain experiences the workplace and educational institutions first and foremost as a social system.

- *Weathering* refers to the constant stress of dealing with racism that can lead to adverse health outcomes for racially marginalized people.

- Racial trauma is more insidious at work and school because these are places in which we spend the majority of our time.

- Trauma teaches us survival skills to keep us safe in a world of harm.

"Racism is a socially transmitted disease passed down through generations."

– *American Academy of Pediatrics*

9

CODE-SWITCHING BY
ANOTHER NAME

"I was learning how to make myself digestible. . .
I wasn't being my authentic self."

– Amadla Stenberg

I was born in Haiti but raised in the United States. Although my first languages were French and Haitian Kreyol, English soon became my primary language.

My parents continued to speak to me in Kreyol, but I was not required to respond in kind. It was encouraged but never forced. Therefore, at home and on Sundays at our Haitian church, you could hear a mixture of Kreyol and English, or what we call Krenglish.

I'm aware that the way I speak English isn't the same way that I speak Kreyol. There is something so distinct about language and how culture gets embedded in it. If you speak multiple languages, sometimes it's easy to transition from one to another, while, other times, it can be awkward, and the translation is insufficient.

This switch between languages is known as *code-switching*. It's traditionally a linguistic term that describes how one alternates between two or more languages.

Code-switching also has another meaning. It's a term adopted by the Black American community that can be traced back to the time of enslavement, when enslaved people had to modify their behavior for survival.

As an unfree person, you couldn't speak freely or act in a way that could be perceived as proud or dignified by White individuals. Keeping one's head bowed, using broken speech, and maintaining a lowly disposition were what was expected. Anything contrary to this would be met with severe repercussions. If you were fortunate enough to have some education and could read, you had to hide your intelligence.

Being forced to present this way created a double life for the enslaved Black person—that of an enslaved person physically and that of the free person they were in their mind.

Code-switching is commonly known as the way a Black person will modify their tone, cadence, speech, hair, attire, and even the way they walk to protect themselves to minimize a White person's bias.

This code-switching behavior is transgenerational. A skill adapted from trauma and used as a form of protection has been passed down through the eras of chattel slavery, Jim Crow, and Civil Rights, and it is still present today.

MASKING

As a clinician, I recognize that the term code-switching is inadequate. Although the definition of the term has been extended beyond simply switching from one language to another, it cannot fully encompass the emotional component behind this switch.

A better term for this modified behavior is *masking*.

Masking is a term used by neurodivergent people and attributed to those diagnosed with Autism Spectrum Disorder or ADHD. It's an umbrella term for camouflaging, compensating, and adaptive morphing—suppressing one's true self.

Masking is how neurodivergent people navigate a neurotypical world. They may mimic social behaviors that are deemed more "socially acceptable" in neurotypical culture.

Some examples of masking are:

- Forcing eye contact.
- Imitating facial expressions and gestures.
- Copying body language or tone.
- Internalizing sensory discomfort.
- Suppressing stimming (self-stimulating behaviors). These are repetitive behaviors such as rocking, whistling, and tapping.
- Pretending to understand or follow a conversation.
- Rehearsing or scripting conversations.
- Suppressing the desire to discuss intense interests (or hyperfixations).

Neurodivergent people mask to protect themselves from discrimination and harassment. They are aware of the stigma around certain disabilities, so they mask in order to not have their disability "outed," or exposed.

Masking is a survival strategy that increases your hypervigilance, contributing to adverse health outcomes such as anxiety, stress, depression, identity loss, "imposter syndrome," PTSD, burnout, and suicidal ideation.

It can involve any behavior that is to the detriment of your authentic self. If it causes you to dissociate from, dismiss, and minimize your feelings for the comfort of others, then it is a form of self-abandonment.

Not being free or safe to be your authentic self can damage your mental health.

> **Not being free or safe to be your authentic self can damage your mental health.**

Although Black Americans have co-opted the term code-switching, what they are experiencing is a hybrid of both. In their masking, they can also be code-switching. Weaving in and out of AAVE (African American Vernacular English) and Standard American English is code-switching; however, putting on a different personality or identity to hide aspects of yourself and your culture while at school or in the workplace is masking.

Masking and EQ

There has been a lack of awareness about how systemic racism and other systems of oppression affect the everyday lives of people who've been marginalized. For example, many are unaware of the masking and code-switching behaviors of many marginalized people.

We learned in Part One that emotional intelligence is the act of knowing, understanding, and responding to emotions within yourself and others. It's the ability to be in tune with yourself and your emotions and to be able to "read the room."

Historically underrepresented people practice a higher degree of social awareness and relationship management when moving through predominantly White, male, neurotypical, and heterosexual environments. As members of a minority group, they often are "reading the room" to determine how safe it is. We've just read how, historically, Black people showing up as their authentic selves has proven dangerous for them.

Black people have learned to understand White individuals' emotions, mannerisms, and characteristics to help them assimilate into the dominant culture without reciprocation.

I've stated before that emotional intelligence is a strength skill. However, there are times we don't want to be strong. Resilience can be tiring. Exhausted by the heavy lifting of moving through the world based only on how the world wants to see you and not necessarily how you authentically want to be seen.

There's an emotional tax that is levied every single time Black people enter predominantly White spaces. If you're the only one in the room, even though you don't want to be the representative of a whole group, you realize that you may become the spokesperson.

W.E.B. Du Bois called this experience *double consciousness*, because there was this peculiar sense of always looking at oneself through the eyes of others. He stated that, as a Black person born in North America, one is born in "*a world which yields to no true self-consciousness, but only lets him see himself through the revelation of the other world.*"

When you know that you are being seen through the lens of stereotypes, prejudices, and biases, you act differently. You don't want to be perceived as the stereotypical angry Black woman or the aggressive Black man who's intimidating and unsafe.

To avoid this predicament, they silence themselves while screaming inside, swallowing their cries so as not to trigger what many in the Black community know as "white tears" or "white rage." One gentleman stated that as the only Black man on his work team, his goal was to be as invisible as possible. Many Black people code-switch to minimize the likelihood of an unfavorable exchange.

You learn to ignore or dismiss hurt feelings for the sake of the individuals who assault you. There's an increase in your social awareness while your emotional awareness is lowered, because the environment isn't one where it's safe for you to acknowledge and regulate your feelings. Therefore, you mute and bury them with the hope you can address them later.

We've seen examples of this during the 2020 vice-presidential debates between Kamala Harris and Mike Pence, and during the hearing of Justice Ketanji Brown Jackson. Both women had to maintain their composure in the face of contempt.

On the contrary, we saw White men like Brett Kavanaugh during his hearing, and women like Megan McCain as a co-host on the show, The View, be able to freely express a broad spectrum of emotions, including anger and frustration, without consequence.

HOW WAS IT TAUGHT

From a young age, Black children have learned to constantly "read the room" because they're hyper-aware of how they are being perceived.

In Chapter 6, we talked about our emotional narratives, where we first learned about feelings and how we and others express them. Those belonging to racially marginalized groups learn at a young age that their feelings are less valid than those of their White counterparts. They witness how their White classmates are extended grace while they are subjected to harsher discipline.

Black parents know this, and because they do, they try to equip their children to face the cruel reality that racism has created. Parents and guardians of Black children in the United States have *The Talk*—a "coming of age" conversation about how to wield their emotional intelligence to stay safe in a world that views them as less than and as a threat.

This talk allows parents to explain to their children the dangers they may face due to racism and what to do and how to compose themselves when encountering law enforcement and other authoritative figures.

What can you do when your color can be used as a weapon against you? You try your best to decrease the fear and discomfort of the other person while holding in all your anxiety, hurt, and pain. You are taught what you can and cannot do. How you can and cannot move.

"Don't wear a hoodie." – Trayvon Martin.

"Don't show signs of being autistic." – Elijah McClain

"Don't play with a toy gun." – Tamir Rice

"Having to spend my childhood rehearsing for the day a police officer would pull me over may sound scary. And I'm aware it's not something parents of all races feel the need to teach their kids. But the day it actually happened, I was grateful, at least, that my mom made sure I was ready." – Riley Lockheart

Lisa Savage, LCSW, CEO of The Center of Child Development, helps Black parents understand that appropriate expressions of emotion are not always disrespectful. She said that these conversations are challenging because within Black culture, we've been trained to believe that our kids must show up a certain way for fear of what could happen when that child goes to school and expresses natural emotions of frustration or disappointment.

How is the teacher, the administrator, or law enforcement going to receive our child's feelings?

Savage educates parents on how racism and White supremacy have shown up in our lives and how that's impacted how we parent. She believes many parents of Black and brown children have experienced the hurt of microaggressions and overt racism. Through their efforts to try to shield them from being stereotyped, they unintentionally end up limiting their children's expressions of emotions and natural curiosity because they fear for their child and how they will be perceived and consequently treated.

When talking with parents, she asks them about how they experience their emotions and whether they allow themselves a full range of emotional experiences, because their kids are going to model what they're showing them. "So really trying, from a family system perspective, to increase the emotional intelligence and emotional literacy within families."

White Preference

Daily, many Black individuals show up as dysfunctional versions of themselves in order to have functional relationships in predominantly White spaces. Granted, the consequences of showing up as one's authentic self will not necessarily cost you your life as it could in the past, when being lynched, brutally beaten, or sold off was a reality. There's still this fear of potentially losing one's livelihood, though, in terms of, "Will I still have a job? Will I still be in this group? Will they hire me if I wear my hair a certain way? What if I don't conform to what is 'expected' of me?"

A 2021 study by the Journal of Experimental Social Psychology highlighted how White people prefer for their Black colleagues to code-switch, or to do what we know now as masking.

I know what you are thinking. *"No way, Farah! Say it ain't so!"*

Oh, it's so. Here's the thing: they don't know that it's code-switching. For instance, many of you just learned about the term code-switching while reading this book. Before, they may have considered Black people who emulate White behavior to be emulating professional behavior.

"There's a difference between malicious intent and people who are conditioned to believe how they behave is the standard," states Marlana Baylis-Ruffin, Life Coach & Tech Consultant.

Do you recall that I encouraged you to consider whom we deem experts at the beginning of this book? Now, I ask you, who defines what's professional?

Historically, the predominant group in the professional workplace and many institutions in the United States was men, specifically White men. These spaces were designed for and with them in mind. What we consider our norms and standards for not only professionalism but also how we define beauty, intelligence, and psychology, among other things, are based on the perspectives and ideologies of White males. Therefore, when we conduct studies created to uncover White participants' perceptions, we cannot be surprised when there are preferences.

Overall, White participants perceived that the "code-switching" Black coworker was more professional than the non-code-switching Black coworker. In contrast, the Black participants perceived that the non-code-switching Black coworker was more professional than the White participants. This would suggest that Black people value and recognize Black cultural norms as professional, unlike their White peers.

In the study, White women deemed straightened hairstyles as the most professional. This is why other Black women praised Michelle Obama for her decision to wear braids at her White House portrait unveiling. This choice to wear her hair in this style was significant because it brought representation to the Black community. Far too many Black women have been told that wearing their hair in natural styles that are common within Black culture was not appropriate nor appreciated.

There are other studies that label Black women who don natural hairstyles as incompetent and aggressive. This preference for straight and more Eurocentric hairstyles is discriminatory and has impacted hiring practices. For this reason, the CROWN Act was created, a law that permits Black people to wear their hair in its natural state at any school or workplace.

The question is, as White people increase their awareness of how systemic racism affects Black and other racialized people's everyday lives—knowing that they are masking—would they evaluate the person differently?

I'd take it a step further and ask not only White people, but *all* of us, whether we recognize that there are members of our society that are masking due to different systems of oppression, and, if so, would we evaluate each other differently?

I've been asked a few times after a presentation whether White people mask in the same way racially marginalized people do. The short answer is no. As I stated previously, masking is a learned practice of survival.

White people do not have a history in which they were considered property, were denied the right to read, get married, or have free will. White people do not have the history of having their culture deemed as less than and uncivilized.

Everywhere they look, they can see themselves and see Whiteness as the norm and the standard. They were not forced to assimilate due to them being the dominant culture.

What would be the purpose of a White person masking or code-switching when they are around non-White people? What would they be protecting themselves from?

To be clear, White people do mask for other reasons, but those reasons pertain to intersectionality, such as is the case with gender or disability. A White woman can mask in the presence of an aggressive or dominating man to protect herself from harm. As I stated earlier, a neurodivergent person who happens to be White may mask when around neurotypical people.

However, if a White person were to linguistically code-switch, only using AAVE when speaking to Black people, for example, saying "Hey, giiiirl!" or "Whatup, homie?" or some trending colloquialism, it would be disingenuous and perceived as racist behavior. White people choosing to hide parts of their Whiteness and mimicking Black culture is not a survival skill, it's appropriation.

HOW DOES IT HARM?

There are many articles about the downsides of emotional intelligence. One argument is that you can be too empathetic, to the point that you become reluctant to ruffle feathers and have a greater aversion to risk.

We aren't operating with high emotional intelligence if we're people-pleasing. This is what we would call conflict avoidance.

However, racially marginalized people avoiding conflict aren't doing so to please others but as a survival mechanism—to preserve and protect their physical and professional well-being.

Black people do so much to try to functionally exist in the United States, viewing their neighbors as fellow human beings, yet they are not being afforded the same respect. The discomfort endured to maintain the majority's comfort is appalling, yet it's understood. Black people are simply trying to live by any means necessary, even if it harms them.

For those who find themselves in the minority, there's often a need to make those who are in the majority, who have disproportionate access to power, feel comfortable. It seems like a necessary thing to do to navigate these spaces; however, it can cause distress to those who must compromise and modify themselves.

When I've explained the unique use of this skillset by Black people in particular, I have been told that this isn't a negative thing and that it highlights resilience, like it's a superpower.

"I don't think there's a superpower out of pain and being marginalized. But I do think there are adaptable skills. And so, I've learned to be adaptable," says Kelley Bonner, LCSW, Company Culture Strategist.

This adaptability allows many to show up for their colleagues in a way that they won't show up for their friends and family because they're exhausted from being patient and empathizing with others who won't do the same in return. It saddens me to watch the personal relationships of some of my Black clients suffer because they don't bring that same level of emotional intelligence to their personal lives.

I remind them that their primary ministry is to their loved ones. To be careful not to give the world the best parts of them and leave their beloved with the crumbs because they are too tired to wield the skill at home.

WHO "BENEFITS?"

One perspective would be that the dominant group benefits when the minority shrinks and assimilates. It keeps them comfortable and allows them not to have to use their emotional intelligence to regulate their discomfort around someone from a minority group exercising their authenticity.

When we have people masking their true selves, we lose the potential for greatness.

When we have people masking their true selves, we lose the potential for greatness.

There's an expression that a chain is only as strong as its weakest link. Please understand that I am not saying that those who have been historically underrepresented are weak; far from it. However, their contributions have been weakened by systems that don't want them to be great.

I mentioned earlier the adverse effects masking has on one's health. This can also cause absenteeism. You will have more children home sick from school and adults not going to work. You will also have increased presenteeism because even when folks show up, they are checked out and disengaged.

This disengagement robs classes and teams of innovation, creativity, and collaboration. You may think all is well, but it could be better. I know it can, and there's plenty of research to back me up. Diverse and inclusive teams are more productive and perform better.

When Black or other racialized people, LGBTQ+ folks, or women hear racist, homophobic, or misogynistic jokes and have to grin through it all, this is really a conversation about making sure others are comfortable at your expense. You're constantly appeasing comfort-seeking people, smiling when they're being inappropriate just so you can get through the day and move on.

Another loss to the majority group is the lack of overall growth and learning. You limit your emotional intelligence if you continue seeking environments that prioritize your comfort. You decrease your chances of building resilience and the skills necessary to self-regulate, be self-aware, and grow in empathy and conflict management. Like a muscle, we cannot grow or get stronger without actively working against resistance.

WHY THIS MATTERS

When people are not free to be their authentic selves because they must compartmentalize, splinter, and fragment themselves, it takes a toll on their mental health and well-being.

In turn, White peers need to acknowledge that the lens through which they approach emotional intelligence is limited by their worldview, which hinders effective use of EQ during social interactions.

-EQ REVIEW-

- *Code-switching* is a linguistic term that explains the transition between two or more languages. It has been adopted by the Black American community and has roots that can be traced back to the time of enslavement, when enslaved people had to modify their behavior for survival.

- *Masking* is a term used within the neurodivergent community that represents how one hides parts of themselves for the comfort of the majority group.

- *Double-Consciousness* is a concept by W.E.B. Du Bois which describes the experience of African Americans feeling the need to have more than one social identity.

- Black people commonly use the term code-switching to explain masking behavior.

- Black people (and other ethnically minoritized groups) can mask and code-switch at the same time.

- Social awareness is the emotional intelligence domain that is elevated when one is masking, and the practice of self-awareness and healthy self-regulation is decreased.

- Studies have found that White people prefer it when Black people code-switch.

- No one truly benefits from people masking because it robs the collective group of creativity, innovation, and collaboration. Also, it hinders the emotional intelligence muscle of the dominant group from being exercised and developed because they get stuck in their comfort zone.

10

PAPERCUTS

"Microaggressions add up. No matter how confident people from marginalized communities feel about their identities, microaggressions create unsafe spaces and make individuals feel like outsiders."

— Mira Yang

Whoever came up with the phrase, "sticks and stones may break my bones, but words will never hurt me," lied. Words do hurt.

How many of you can remember an unkind comment said to you as a child? Whether someone thought it was lighthearted teasing or they were intentionally being mean, you haven't forgotten about it. Shoot! I still haven't forgotten about the time this little boy told me in middle school that I had a big nose!

Many of us still carry these words with us. I can't tell you how often my clients share the harsh or mean-spirited things they were told during childhood. Whether they came from a family member, a classmate, or an adult, these words haven't been forgotten. They left a scar, reminding you that someone was unkind with your heart.

Callous words and actions are like papercuts to our spirit. No one likes a papercut. They happen unexpectedly, slicing one's skin, quickly starting to sting, and sometimes bleeding. This unwelcomed injury is often used to define microaggressions—a death by a thousand (paper) cuts. However, those receiving these cuts know that these wounds aren't always micro—they can be macro and cut deep.

When we read about masking in the previous chapter, we learned that this behavior is taught early. With all that we know about the harmful effects of masking on our mental health, why would anyone continue to do so? It's because there are environments that remind us that we are not accepted. How so? By the occurrence of microaggressions.

Microaggressions are statements or actions regarded as indirect, subtle, intentional, or unintentional discrimination against members of an underrepresented and marginalized group such as a racial or ethnic minority. We may think *small* or *insignificant* when we hear the word *micro*. So, when we consider the word microaggression, we fall prey to the belief that "it's not that big of a deal." However, it is a big deal. Words are powerful and have an impact; we should be mindful of how we use them, especially words that are used to offend and assault.

Additionally, we need to be clear about what aggression we are describing. Is it racist? Sexist? Homophobic? Let's call a thing a thing so we know exactly what we are talking about. We're becoming more emotionally intelligent with each page, so let's practice standing flat-footed and talking about these systems of oppression with our whole chest. Don't worry; I'm right here if you lose your balance.

IMPLICIT BIAS

It is estimated that our brains are exposed to 11 million pieces of information at any given moment. However, our conscious brain can only process about 50 pieces of information at a time. As a result, our brains develop mental shortcuts to help fill those gaps.

Even though cognitive biases are universal, they are not neutral. These gaps are filled by our past experiences, environment, and everything we read, watch, and learn. This subconscious lens forms stereotypes and attitudes, known as **implicit biases**, which shape our beliefs, decisions, and behavior.

These biases cause us to make instant assumptions about situations and people based on characteristics such as race, gender, ethnicity, age, ability, sexuality, or appearance. While stereotypes impact everyone, they are especially harmful to groups that have been marginalized.

Many organizations have done implicit/unconscious bias workshops and training, which have produced little fruit. The problem with doing unconscious bias work is that it can leave us feeling that it is out of our control and not our responsibility when this bias is at play.

The issue isn't unconscious bias; it's *unchecked* bias.

When we don't challenge our thoughts, emotions, and behaviors, we continue to give ourselves license to act recklessly, utterly indifferent to the emotional collateral damages that come from our very words. Unchecked bias occurs when we operate from a position of low emotional intelligence. When we rush to assumptions and judgments, we fail to practice the three A's of awareness, assessment, and action.

The more we increase our emotional intelligence, the more we become aware of these biases. The biases that come from racism need to be checked. I know racism is a word that we don't like. It brings up unpleasant feelings, but we must address it in all its forms: systemic, internalized, and interpersonal.

Unfortunately, microaggressions are commonplace and are experienced by many historically marginalized and underrepresented people daily. Microaggressions, in their verbal or behavioral indignities, communicate hostility and are demeaning toward people, especially those who have been racially marginalized. They can be broken into three categories: microinsults, microinvalidations, and microassaults.

Microinsults

Microinsults are subtle ways of demeaning a person's ethnic heritage or gender. One of the most common microinsults are questions like, "How did you get this job?" or "How did you get into this school or program?" These questions are intentionally insensitive. They imply that the person could not have gotten where they are by their merit, but only by affirmative action or to fill a quota.

Another type of microinsult is choosing not to attempt to pronounce someone's name because it's unfamiliar. Or, worse, calling them by a name you prefer because "it's easier." If someone tells you it's okay to call them a different name, take a moment to consider the reason for this. It's more than likely that they are aware of your discomfort and are trying to make you feel more at ease.

We must also recognize power dynamics. If you are in a senior position and they report to you, or if they are a child and you're the adult, they may give you this pass out of respect. Lastly, many give up because they've gotten tired of hearing their name mispronounced.

Choosing to give a person a nickname or address them by the "American version" of their name shows a lack of respect for their culture and identity. It is interesting to see what names we can pronounce, and the ones we claim are too difficult.

In the last chapter, I mentioned Justice Ketanji Brown Jackson and Vice President Kamala Harris. White media correspondents butchered both women's names, yet, somehow, Galifianakis, Tchaikovsky, and Gyllenhaal are names that are said with ease.

We have esteemed European-sounding names over all others. We see how this microaggression plays out when people apply for jobs. Those with European names are more likely to be called in for an interview than someone whose resume has Sheniqua, Zhāng, or Ranjana at the top. This is how microaggressions perpetuate systemic racism and inequality by creating a sense of racial superiority. The unchecked bias perpetuates a lack of diversity because people choose what is familiar to them.

EQ-Tip

Check your bias. Slow down and recognize how choosing not to attempt to pronounce a person's name shows a lack of social awareness and harms relationships. Imagine introducing yourself at the beginning of a meeting and then being called the wrong name the whole time. It may not bother you, but what if it did? You would feel like those in the room didn't respect or care about you. Take the time to consider how being careless with someone's name impacts them. If you need to, ask for help with pronouncing their name.

There are times that these insults aren't verbal. For example, one non-verbal microinsult is the act of touching someone's hair without permission. Many Black men and women have experienced what could be likened to being at a petting zoo, and they are the pet. If they wear their hair naturally curly, they must prepare for unwanted hands that try to steal a feel.

EQ-Tip

Practice self-control and keep your hands to yourself. Touching someone without their consent crosses boundaries and can be considered assault. Even if you believe that you are doing so as a form of admiration, regulate your emotions so you do not cause distress to another simply because you wanted to see how soft someone's afro was or touch someone's braids.

Historically, Black bodies have been used for entertainment and put on display around the world. Human zoos were popular in the nineteenth and twentieth centuries, exhibiting Black and Indigenous people in cages. These zoos would have guides that described these humans in animalistic terms.

To try to touch someone's hair and pet them as if they are a chia pet, strips them of their agency. If you find yourself getting offended when they physically move away, get angry, or tell you "no," please note that the rudeness isn't on them but on you. Regardless of how "good" your intent may be, your impact is what matters. If you want to make a better connection with your Black coworker, neighbor, student, etc., this isn't the way to go about it.

Microinvalidations

Microinvalidations are subtle ways to exclude, invalidate, or negate someone's experience. In essence, it's a form of gaslighting: it leaves a person questioning their sanity, thoughts, and feelings.

You may be familiar with, "Jeff didn't mean it that way." Another popular phrase is, "I can't be racist because I have a partner/friend/child who is Black."

Stop. Don't be this person. These are statements rooted in defensiveness and an utter lack of accountability.

Men who are misogynists have wives, daughters, sisters, and mothers. Their relationships with women have not caused them to think critically or change their beliefs. They continue to believe that women are not equal to them and can be treated with contempt—it's the same thing with race or sexuality. Your proximity to a Black person doesn't make you less anti-Black. Your proximity to a gay person does not make you less homophobic. Using someone who identifies with the group you are attacking should not be a scapegoat for your poor behavior and low emotional intelligence.

Another form of microinvalidation that often occurs in the workplace is when two people of the same ethnicity are mistaken for one another. Two Latino men worked at the same office. One had a bald head with a mustache and beard, while the other had a darker complexion and a full head of hair. Frequently, these men were called by each other's names. This leaves one to question whether they were being seen for who they are individually.

Some microinvalidations occur when any aspect of a person's identity other than their disability is ignored or denied. "I can't believe you are married," and "She must be with him because of money," are some of the comments Shane Burcaw and Hannah Aylward often receive.

Shane has spinal muscular atrophy (SMA) and uses a wheelchair. He and his wife are an inter-abled couple. These comments question the validity of the marriage because, for some, it is hard to picture someone living a "normal" life outside of their disability, as if those with certain physical disabilities aren't attractive or don't warrant love.

What makes us think these things, or, worse, say them aloud or post them on social media? It's our lack of self-control and awareness. We point out things we don't understand, and because they seem too different, we don't take the time to investigate our thoughts and regulate our feelings. We simply react, and to make it easier and more comfortable for ourselves, we label these differences as wrong. Doing so lets us off the hook from having to empathize with the other person because we have jailed them with our judgment.

Microassaults

A microassault is a type of overt discrimination, using racially inflammatory language and insults expressed intentionally to a person of a marginalized group. This includes name-calling, using epithets, and referring to someone as "colored" or "Oriental." It can also arise in the form of discouraging interracial interactions, such as a White waiter deliberately serving another White patron before a Black or Asian person. Displaying a swastika to intimidate others is another example. Microassaults are similar to what has been called "old-fashioned" racism. That's right, folks, racism has been here long enough that there are new and old versions of it!

Let's think about this for a moment. Again, I want to encourage us all to examine our words. Words matter, and they need to make sense. If you intentionally use the N-word to cause harm, there's nothing "small" about that! So why do we call it microassault? Doing so devalues its impact on the assaulted.

WORK AND SCHOOL

Covid-19 pushed us into a virtual workplace that many of us did not anticipate. While we have made and continue to make adjustments around remote work, there's a benefit to working from home as a person of a systemically excluded group—you don't have to deal with the microaggressions of "office culture."

Even when it shows up in video calls, there's now an option to turn off your camera or log off and not interact with those who perpetuate or commit microaggressions—something you would have to do at the office.

When the news is particularly distressing due to racial incidents or violence towards marginalized communities, there's less pressure to pretend that everything is okay and you don't have to deal with superficial offers of support that come with being in the office.

Whether you're remote or in-office, you can still be impacted by microaggressions from coworkers or classmates, asking you to speak on behalf of an entire community when news that impacts a certain community begins to trend.

After several incidents of anti-Asian violence, I had several Asian clients tell me that they were asked to share their feelings about these events.

Their White leaders and colleagues wanted them to tell personal stories of their experience with racism, believing it would benefit the group, that it would garner empathy.

When these requests are made, there's no consideration for the person who shares their grief and racial trauma. There's no assurance of psychological or emotional safety. More often than not, there aren't trained experts available in case the retelling of their trauma triggers not only the person, but others who are present.

If one is not careful, this activity has the potential to be careless and callous instead of caring and compassionate.

Many declined as they recognized that participating in this type of vulnerability was for the benefit of their White colleagues and not for their healing. It was trauma porn, an opportunity to exploit racial trauma in the name of a "DEI Healing Circle."

CULTURAL AWARENESS

There's a mental exercise in decoding the majority's comments and behavior. You do your best to use your "Spidey-Social-Awareness-Sense" to decipher whether a statement is a racist, sexist, ableist microaggression, or simply a comment at face value.

Unfortunately, many Black people in predominantly White spaces aren't awarded the luxury of giving or receiving the benefit of the doubt.

There's an accusation of being aggressive, confrontational, or not being a "team player" simply because someone doesn't respond in the way their White colleagues or peers feel is acceptable. Policing of tone and behavior falls under the guise of constructive feedback; however, it's a push for them to be more White-presenting.

Beverly is a tall Jamaican woman with a dark complexion, a toothy smile, and a big personality. She's witty and confident and knows her way around the banking industry. Despite her expertise and relationship management skills, she has been told on more than one occasion that she's intimidating and should "tone it down" during presentations.

"I use my hands often when I talk, and my voice gets elevated when I'm passionate about something."

I can relate as a Caribbean woman; I know how animated some of us can be. As we learned in the last chapter, there's a specific way in which some White people feel one should comport themselves in the workplace—and that way is *their* way, because it is familiar.

If they had used emotional intelligence, Beverly's leaders and colleagues would have led with curiosity instead of accusations that weren't accurate. Her passion is seen as aggression, when, in reality, they are the ones aggressing.

These aggressions that are used to depict a Black woman inconsiderately can derail and delay her career progression.

EQ-Tip

Social Awareness: If you have colleagues or students that are of a different race, ethnicity, or culture than you, make an effort to learn more about their cultural norms so that you don't mislabel or miscategorize them.

Self-Awareness: If there's a behavior or tone that feels off-putting for you, practice the three A's. Take a moment to be aware of your feelings, assess what is triggering your emotions, and then try your best to respond in a productive manner.

Self-Management: Leading with curiosity can help you regulate your feelings. The more you can understand where the other person is coming from and why they do what they do, this information can help you manage your feelings and increase your empathy.

THE RACE CARD

"Stop using the race card." You've heard this racial aggression before. Please tell me who purposely applied for this fictitious card with real consequences, which has an emotional tax so excessive that all who've been issued the card would've preferred to have been declined.

Race is a social construct, and it's one that wasn't built by the hands of those who have been racially marginalized. It's funny that the issuer of said "race card" gets irritated whenever the card is used. Perhaps we wouldn't be where we are today if this card was never created, and we weren't left paying this high interest rate that continues to accumulate.

You see, this invisible card that magically gets placed in the wallets and purses of racially marginalized people isn't like the typical Black Card. Albeit exclusive, it doesn't have perks. The irony is how the actual Black Card is the ultimate status symbol, while the imaginary one symbolizes your status for being a Black person. Those who carry this card are reminded that they are card-carrying members by the microaggressions they must deal with daily.

Trust me. No one wants to play this race card; it's always in the deck.

IMPOSTER SYNDROME

I often say, don't internalize an external narrative that doesn't serve you. There are many messages and narratives that society tells us about ourselves. Whether they contain internalized racism, misogyny, ableism, or inflexible gender roles, these stories can harm our psychological and emotional well-being.

Experienced enough times, these slights can cause one to experience what is now a popular term—imposter syndrome. It's a feeling of inadequacy or incompetence. You doubt that you belong in the room despite objective success, your accomplishments, education, and experience, causing you to work harder because you feel that you must prove yourself. You wade through the ever-rising waters of perfectionism while simultaneously dismissing any positive affirmations or attributing your success to luck rather than talent.

Imposter syndrome doesn't allow you to have an adequate view of yourself.

The feedback you receive from these microaggressions is used to distort whatever perception you may have of yourself. Even with accolades and achievements, these experiences leave you questioning yourself, asking, "I wonder if. . .?"

I wonder if I'm actually qualified. I wonder if they hired me because I think out of the box—or was I hired to help them check a box?

TO BE COLOR BLIND

"I don't see color!"

We've heard this statement before. It either stumbles out defensively from someone with good intentions or is blurted out defiantly by someone trying to disprove their racism.

Let's unpack this statement and its impact from an emotionally intelligent lens. Are you ready to put on your critical thinking caps? I know that there might be an urge to get defensive or practice cognitive dissonance. We know that's your brain trying to protect you from discomfort, but I encourage you to lean into it.

Ready? Great! Here we go.

For some, saying that you are colorblind or are teaching your children not to see color regarding race may be "well-intended;" however, it shows a lack of critical thinking. We ought to be curious about the intent, but also equally concerned about the impact.

As we grow in our self-awareness and social awareness, we need to receive feedback to show up better. It will help improve our communication and ability to empathize with other perspectives.

When Black people, specifically Black Americans, counter this colorblind statement with, "if you don't see color, you don't see me," that doesn't mean that they've watered down their entire identity to just their skin color. They're saying that to deny their skin color is to deny the historical trauma affixed to it.

Due to the color of their skin, they've been discriminated against, dehumanized, and devalued. To ignore systemic racism is to ignore a part of the Black experience. Also, to deny color is to deny the beauty of ethnic and cultural differences.

Ideally, a colorblind society, in sociology, would be one in which racial classification does not affect a person's opportunities or status. This race-neutral society would govern free from differential legal or social treatment based on someone's race or color. The goal would be genuine equality. We aren't there yet, though. So, in the meantime, let's consider how our words affect others.

How can we better listen to the correction we receive when we have misstepped? How can we improve on being more curious about our thoughts and hearts as we engage with those different from us? It's more than appearing like a good person; to *be* a good person, you must be willing to continue practicing accountability, humility, apology, and grace.

We cannot lower our emotional intelligence meter when actively striving for healthier relationships. We must elevate all the domains to see ourselves and others more clearly. It may be uncomfortable when someone corrects us, but how else are we going to learn? If you genuinely desire equality and equity, diversity can't be excluded. This means you must include diverse voices in your learning.

Continuing to use this colorblind statement is to be willfully stubborn and unkind. You are choosing to be insensitive, to ignore how this statement is hurtful and harmful—ignoring the voices of those who try to educate you on why seeing them and their **hue**manity is important.

ALL LIVES MATTER?

We cannot have a chapter on microaggressions and not address "All Lives Matter." Colorblind walked so that All Lives Matter could soar. This slogan has become a low emotional intelligence rebuttal to Black Lives Matter.

To be clear, I am not talking about the Black Lives Matter movement; I am only addressing the affirmation, because that is what it is: an affirmation. It affirms the humanity and personhood of Black lives.

The statement does not degrade, devalue, or dismiss the lives of other races and ethnicities. It advocates for the lives that have been histori-cally degraded, devalued, and dismissed.

When one hears the words "Black lives matter," whether it's shouted during a protest, written on a screen, emblazoned on someone's t-shirt, or painfully whispered after witnessing racial injustice, it's interesting that, out of the abundance of one's heart, one's mouth would say: "All lives matter."

If we are honest with ourselves, there should have never been a necessity for the statement, "Black Lives Matter." However, we live in a broken world where everyone doesn't view all lives equally. The response of "All Lives Matter" is a knee-jerk response.

Let's walk the dog for a minute. What is the emotion behind the All Lives Matter rebuttal? Is it fear? Is it disgust? I ask because, at face value, it sounds like an inclusive statement, yet it comes off as very angry, aggressive, and not empathetic at all. It's a microaggression that is meant not to include Black lives but to quiet their voices.

We can also test the genuineness of this statement as well. All Lives Matter quickly led to Blue Lives Matter. This was an interesting shift. We were no longer talking about people; we were talking about a voca-tion. This new rebuttal valued the lives of police officers above the lives of Black citizens—and even that's disingenuous, because Blue Lives don't seem to matter when it's a Black officer out of uniform that is killed.

Listen, when October rolls around, and we see sports teams wear-ing pink and companies and organizations highlighting breast cancer awareness, we don't get angry and cry out, "All cancers matter." Why? Because we know that all cancers matter. During this particular month, we are bringing awareness to a specific cancer. We'd consider someone shouting "All cancers matter!" or "What about prostate cancer?" to be extremely insensitive. Yet, somehow, some of us deem All Lives Matter acceptable.

It's a response that doesn't take accountability for its negative implications. It's based on a narrative that perpetuates the idea that lives that are not White should not be heard, seen, validated, or dignified.

Perhaps for some of you, this is unsettling.

If so, I encourage you to ask yourself, "Do I disagree because of my emotions, or because of facts?"

Once again, I implore you to use your "thinking brains" and practice asking yourselves questions before you react. This is how you check your biases.

You may feel discomfort realizing that saying "All Lives Matter" is rooted in racism, specifically, anti-Blackness. People don't want to believe that because they want to be seen as "being good." They want the appearance of not being stained by racism or malice. This desire to distance ourselves from the root of our biases leads us to practice cognitive dissonance.

Emotional intelligence requires us to practice "the pause" and to challenge and reflect on the emotions that come up for us. We can be honest that this doesn't make us feel comfortable. Self-auditing helps us to process the discomfort. We can easily slip into cognitive dissonance if we don't challenge our thoughts and emotions.

Cognitive dissonance allows us to live with a lie, which has us forfeit the domains of self-awareness and self-regulation for our comfort. This goes back to Sarah Noll Wilson's comment about self-awareness being convenient when it's comfortable and only put into practice to reinforce a level of comfort. If something feels offensive or unpleasant, that's your intuition telling you to check yourself.

It takes self-management and empathy to hear and understand something about a group you are not a part of and not try to make it about you. When you take over the conversation, redirecting the focus and empathy from the intended recipient to yourself, that's called centering.

Instead, take that energy spent being offended to listen. Also, don't evoke your tears. This is a defensive move used in hopes of deflecting.

In an interview for the podcast We Can Do Hard Things, Dr. Yaba Blay makes a poignant point regarding White women's tears. They are quick to be used to garner empathy from onlookers, yet the tears of Black women don't move others to that same level of compassion.

The Strong Black Woman is not a compliment but a constraint, a snare to trap Black women to keep them from being free to express their emotions and live a liberated human existence.

I'm reminded of a James Baldwin quote: "People can cry much easier than they can change." These tears are used to wash away and absolve them from taking responsibility for the harm they've caused. In return, the racially aggressed must be resilient and maintain their composure.

WHY THIS MATTERS

Theresa M. Robinson, DEI and Anti-Racism Educator and Speaker, says it best: "Microaggressions are a multi-sensory experience for those on the receiving end of them."

They can be read in facial expressions and felt in the unwelcoming energy in a room. One can sense being othered, and hate has a scent that can be detected.

Microaggressions aren't always small, and they are never harmless. Enduring a lifetime of them can be devastating to your mental health. When we have numerous members of our society who live on the receiving end of various aggressions and assaults, the compound effect is like an infection in the body. Each aggression weakens our immune system and breaks down the body that we call society.

The trauma we experience from microaggressions teaches us to use emotional intelligence strategically for our safety but not necessarily for our peace. As such, it is imperative for historically marginalized people to care for our own well-being. In the next chapter, I provide the self-care tools needed to help minimize the effects of aggressions on one's health.

Unfortunately, one can't have complete healing, as these systems and -isms are all around us and will continue to harm. Our pursuit of peace must be our act of resistance.

-EQ REVIEW-

- The practice of masking occurs because of environments that remind marginalized individuals that they are not accepted through the occurrence of microaggressions.

- The gaps in our knowledge of others that are filled by our past experiences, environment, and everything we read, watch, and learn allow for the formation of stereotypes and attitudes, known as **implicit bias.**

- Microaggressions are statements or actions that are instances of indirect, subtle, intentional, or unintentional discrimination against members of an underrepresented and marginalized group, such as a racial or ethnic minority.

- There are three types of microaggressions: microinsults, microinvalidations, and microassaults.

  o Microinsults are subtle ways of demeaning a person's ethnic heritage or gender.

  o Microinvalidations are subtle ways of excluding, invalidating, or negating the experience of someone.

  o Microassaults are a type of overt discrimination, using racially inflammatory language and insults expressed intentionally to a person belonging to a marginalized group.

- Race is a social construct that wasn't built by the hands of those who have been racially marginalized.

- Experiencing microaggressions daily can cause one to experience imposter syndrome.

- Statements like "I'm colorblind" and "All Lives Matter" are microaggressions.

- Microaggressions aren't always small, and they are never harmless.

11

SELF-CARE FOR HISTORICALLY MARGINALIZED PEOPLE

*"Caring for myself is not self-indulgence; it is self-preservation,
and that is an act of political warfare."*

— *Audre Lorde*

Don't skip over this chapter.

Although I've titled this *Self-Care for Historically Marginalized People*,
that doesn't mean that if you aren't an individual within any of those
groups, you can't benefit from reading this.

Self-care is something that we all can learn and improve on. Also, I'm
inviting you to read this chapter to continue to grow your curiosity and
compassion for others. You now have access to a great resource you
can share!

We tend to think of self-care as a luxury, something that we'll get to
when we "have time" or "when everything else is done," but self-care
is a necessity.

I define self-care as the intentional daily act of creating a life you don't want to run away from. The action must be intentional, otherwise, as my colleague Melissa Douglass, LCSW, says, "delayed self-care becomes self-rescue." Read that again.

> **I define self-care as the intentional daily act of creating a life you don't want to run away from.**

When we're constantly in survival mode, we don't realize how much we're not fully living. I love the Mental Health Alliance B4Stage4 philosophy, which reminds us that we don't want to wait until Stage 4 to address cancer; the same preventative practice is needed when caring for our mental health and overall well-being.

We cannot exercise emotional intelligence well if we aren't implementing healthy self-care practices. If you're tired and worn out, you cannot operate at your highest level. Recall what we've learned about how our brain processes thoughts and feelings.

A stressed brain will have difficulty regulating itself. Our emotional brain and brainstem become active and take over. This decreases the use of the prefrontal cortex, throwing rational and logical thinking out the window. When we're stressed and pressed, we regress.

At the same time, we cannot successfully practice self-care without emotional intelligence. Being aware of what we enjoy and what energizes us encourages us to implement time to engage with these activities and people. This way, you can intelligently structure your life and create a better alignment for yourself when you know what fuels and drains you.

How should you use emotional intelligence as part of your self-care when you are part of a historically and systemically marginalized group? As we've read, many have learned to use this skill to navigate predominantly White, hetero, male, and ableist spaces but have not applied it well in their personal lives.

Emotional intelligence can be used as a self-care tool to cultivate healthy relationships, set necessary boundaries, make assertive use of our voices, and adequately hold space to acknowledge and process emotions—especially those feelings that surface when experiencing systemic trauma. In this chapter, I will provide tips and tools that you can implement immediately to improve your mental health and well-being.

There needs to be a setting aside of the notion that you must grin and bear experiences of microaggressions. Or that you must shut up and be grateful for having a good job, a lovely house, or whatever else society tries to gaslight you with, as if you aren't thankful for these things. You can sit in the seat of gratitude while acknowledging that the chair is broken. It's not biting the hand that feeds you but knowing that what you are being fed are leftovers or remnants that have spoiled.

What does this mean? It means you are tired of sitting in an uncomfortably crooked seat, trying to make it look straight. It also means that you work hard for what's on your plate, and what's given still leaves you hungry. You don't complain because you're just trying to live, but, the question is, is this a healthy way to live? No, it isn't. What can you do so that you can move beyond existing? So that you can be, do, and live well? You must care for yourself even if the world seems as if it doesn't care for you.

ELEVATE YOUR OWN AWARENESS

Minda Harts, author and workplace and equity consultant, stated that, to write her best-selling books *The Memo* and *Right Within*, she had to lean into her own emotional intelligence. These books address a Black woman's experience within corporate America and healing from racial trauma in the workplace.

Harts reflects on the times that she'd dealt with racial hostility and offensive behavior inside of a meeting, upset that no one said or did anything. However, years later, she ponders on where colleagues were emotionally and whether they even had the tools to show up emotionally for her.

> "That really keeps me from not being bitter and resentful because I realize that people don't have the emotional intelligence that they need to even tap into what's going on. And that's why I decided, if so-and-so doesn't have emotional intelligence, I still can be right within."

Please note that such awareness does not remove the hurt, anger, or disappointment you may feel after you've been discriminated against or harassed, but reflecting on the possibility that the bystanders' inaction could be caused by their own emotional narratives can help to regulate your emotions.

You can still acknowledge the harm and hold people accountable, yet not get stuck in your pain.

Minda says it best, "Our lives depend on it. Our longevity, our sustainability depends on our self-regulation; our emotional intelligence."

REST

I'm aware that there are challenges to practicing self-care among marginalized folks, specifically Black people. This group, whose emotions have been commonly ignored, has also learned to ignore their feelings in the name of resilience. Who has time to think about feelings when you are trying to survive? To bear the pain brought on by chattel slavery, one had to have thick skin in more ways than one. Pain does that.

Where there are wounds, there's tenderness covered by new skin. I'm urging you to dress these wounds properly. The strong Black man and woman trope has been more of a disservice in its use by both Black and non-Black individuals, having turned into a banner to continue to demand their labor.

So, telling you to use emotional intelligence as self-care is radical because there's a vile message that society tells you that it's not okay to fully feel. To be human. If you are to feel, those emotions are invalid. I'm imploring you to take time to be aware of your emotions and to feel them. Practice emotional awareness and mindfulness. Recognize and name your emotions and listen to what your body is telling you.

Often, women struggle with resting. Everyone else can rest while they serve. It's a juggling act where all the balls must stay in the air. That there's no time for rest lest the balls drop. My dear, let them fall as you lay. You can pick them back up later.

Despite popular belief, rest is productive. It allows your brain to reboot. It will enable your body to reset and give you the energy to show up as your best self. Because you've rested, you are less likely to be reactive, so you can respond constructively. Rest will prove to help improve your mood and increase your innovation and creativity. You will feel grounded and have more clarity.

SET BOUNDARIES – SAY NO

Practicing emotionally intelligent self-care means knowing when we've hit our capacity.

It's okay to say "no." Not a "no, and," or a "no, but." "No" is a complete sentence—no need for commas.

Not everyone will be happy with your boundaries, especially if they are boundary violators. Boundary violators make you feel bad for honoring your "no" while having no problem imposing their "no" upon you. They will find ways to manipulate your emotions to turn your no into a "yes." Don't let them.

It's important to know when and where to set boundaries and with whom. Just because you are accessible doesn't mean you are available.

Leave environments that drain you. Minimize your participation in conversations or functions that elevate your stress or are triggering.

Another thing. Just because they asked you to lead the Diversity, Equity, and Inclusion efforts at your organization doesn't mean that you should.

Yep, I said it.

Don't get me wrong; I understand why you said "yes." This is important work! You have this beautiful desire to help and a vision of how you could change the world. . . Well, maybe not the whole world, but definitely change your organization for the better.

But it's hard to be the advocate and the abused.

But it's hard to be the advocate and the abused.

Sometimes we find ourselves experiencing unnecessary stress because we keep saying "yes" to the good instead of "yes" to what's right for us. This reminds me of the verse, "*everything is permissible, but not everything is beneficial.*" Just because you can, doesn't mean you should.

Often, you are asked to participate or lead the charge simply because of your race, gender, sexual orientation, or disability. No consideration is given to your actual knowledge or expertise in this area. You check the box. You represent a marginalized group. Therefore, you should lead the DEI work and discussion.

False.

You do not have to put your lived experience on display to teach people how to be more compassionate or to acknowledge your humanity.

EQ-Tip

Three things to consider before entering (or while in) a DEI role:

1. Have you processed your race-based or [insert other historically/systemically oppressed group] trauma with a therapist?

2. How good are you at setting boundaries?

3. Do you have a place to process your emotions when you get triggered?

4. Will you have support to get the work done?

5. Will you have the authorization to be successful: alignment with and buy-in from senior management?

Numbers 1-3 are essential, as they help you assess your self-care plan before diving into this career path.

I've watched individuals move into this role without considering how their unprocessed trauma would impact how they showed up and how it would affect their work. Get on someone's physical or virtual couch ASAP if you haven't worked with a therapist to address these issues.

SOCIAL MEDIA DETOX

Engaging with social media can yield higher rates of depression and anxiety. It can become overwhelming when the news becomes loaded with traumatic events that impact a marginalized or underrepresented group.

Since 2020, COVID-19 has highlighted a pandemic that was already present: the pandemic of racism. Our newsfeed has been filled with the uncertainty caused by a health crisis, anti-Asian hate, transphobia, and videos of unarmed Black people being murdered at the hands (and knees) of police officers. The news cycle has been exhausting.

A study published in 2018 by Jacob Bor from Boston University's School of Public Health stated that each exposure to a killing of a Black person was associated with an average of four poor mental health days for Black respondents, with a maximum of fourteen poor mental health days. Now imagine if more than one incident occurs within the month! We now have a person who is managing the stress of vicarious trauma while having to show up at their workplaces or classrooms as if they are unaffected.

Here are some ways to create boundaries to minimize racial stress caused by social media:

- Use filters
- Take a social media break
- Turn off notifications
- Schedule social media activity
- Temporarily remove apps
- Turn off auto-play

Every post doesn't need to be read, and every post doesn't need your comment. Keep scrolling. The internet is already loud; you don't need to add your voice and increase the volume. Engaging can be very tempting, but it often leads to stress.

Don't be a "Captain Save-a-Fool." You can't address all the things. You can acknowledge that what you read was racist/sexist/homophobic/ableist, then keep it moving. Preserve your time and peace. Take a moment to assess if the person on the other end is even open-minded and teachable, and if it will be a constructive conversation. There are some people who are hell-bent on holding on to their biased views of you and others, and you can't change that.

Use your emotional intelligence to regulate your feelings, communicate effectively, and know when to disengage.

JOURNALING

It's essential for our well-being to own our stories. An excellent way to do this is through writing a journal. Journaling helps you to acknowledge that what happened to you was wrong and hurtful.

I want you to be empowered and to give yourself permission to love yourself and not practice self-abandonment by not acknowledging your feelings. Don't tuck your emotions away; process and release them. The practice of journaling is a form of self-advocacy because it allows you to use your voice and describe your feelings.

You can journal in expository form or use bullet points. Whatever the format, the key is to let it come out in a way that helps you process what occurred. If you've experienced discrimination or microaggressions at work, the store, at school, or wherever, write it down. Get it out of you.

After you've written about what transpired, you can reframe and reappraise the experience. I will keep saying this until you get it: don't internalize an external narrative. That experience of hate and ignorance does not define you, nor does it have to be your story.

Also, journaling can help increase your emotional awareness. It can help you discover and express your thoughts and emotions, and to become more aware of what you are experiencing and better understand who you are.

I'm aware that some of you may have past trauma or an upbringing that prevented you from expressing a range of emotions safely. Journaling through those feelings helps you to recognize that emotions like sadness or anger aren't inherently bad. These are natural emotions, and you are safe to feel these things.

Lastly, journaling provides you with receipts, otherwise known as documentation. When approaching your human resource department,

you can reference your journal entries if needed. Document everything you can. Save the emails, the memos, all of it.

CALL IN. . .

You may be familiar with the phrase "calling in sick." I encourage you
to call in Black. Or Asian. Or LGBT+, or Muslim—you get the point.

When your community is under attack, you may need to take a mental
health day (or days) to process injustice. If witnessing certain injustices
equates to multiple poor mental health days, people need the time and
space to process them. Work isn't always the safest place to do that.

EQ-Tip

If you are not part of the marginalized group that is dealing with
a traumatic event and you have not had any meaningful interactions, consider these four questions:

- Why am I reaching out to this person?
- Is my inquiry about their well-being genuine and indica-
  tive of our relationship?
- If I've never spoken to this person before, why now?
- Am I wanting to be perceived as good?

Your intentions may be well-meaning, but if you haven't had any
significant communication with this person, this is not the time
for them to deal with deciphering whether your interaction is
genuine or not. This adds extra emotional labor to what they are
already processing.

We'll talk more about good intentions in Part Three.

"I was tired of the fake concern. Coworkers I didn't even know were
sending me emails after Floyd's murder asking me if I was okay. . .

I knew they didn't care. Like, why would I share my pain with you? I don't even know you!" This was the general sentiment of Black employees that I spoke with.

Pre-2020 workplace culture was to leave emotions at the door, but the landscape has changed, and employees are looking for companies with leaders who are empathetic, culturally aware, and understand that team members may need a minute to catch their breath. If you want them to show up well, allow them to recuperate from the pain of seeing people who look like them being harmed and killed due to hate.

ACTIVITIES THAT AFFIRM YOUR ETHNICITY AND CULTURE

Representation matters. When you are the only one of your ethnicity or culture in a specific setting and can't see images of people that look like you or have a similar cultural background, it can negatively impact your well-being.

Read a book, watch a movie or television series, attend a museum or festival, or simply listen to music and enjoy foods that celebrate your culture and heritage. These activities can help reinforce a positive view of yourself and your culture.

CONNECT WITH COMMUNITY

You can't have self-care absent from community. Finding a local or an online group of people going through the same struggles as you can help you feel less alone.

Be intentional about making time to connect with others. This could be planning routine phone calls with friends and family, or activities such as game nights, brunch, or going for walks. You can also join a place of worship, book club or recreational sports team.

Connecting with others gives us a sense of belonging and helps release "feel good" chemicals like oxytocin and endorphins that reward the brain and foster bonding.

Like the *Cheers* theme song, there's something about going somewhere "where everybody knows your name." At the end of the day, it is truly a gift to find a place where you are fully seen and heard without judgment. Go where you are celebrated and feel safe to be your authentic self.

CHANGE YOUR ENVIRONMENT

There's a saying, "Why would you sit at a table that Jesus would have flipped?"

Recognize when environments are safe and when it's time to remove yourself. Every space doesn't need your presence. We don't have to be in every room and seated at every table.

There was a Black Chief Equity Officer of a national nonprofit whose mental health was declining due to the toxicity of her work environment. The organization hired her to improve its DEI efforts. The officer soon realized that all the things she was told when she was hired were resounding gongs and clanging cymbals. What seemed like sincere desires to improve the workplace were lip service and window dressing. Instead of support, she was thrown under the bus at every turn.

She began experiencing increased symptoms of depression and anxiety. After almost three decades in the nonprofit executive leadership space, she reached her breaking point.

She sought advice, and many of her White peers encouraged her to stay, stating that her presence was needed to make a change. That it's a fight at the C-suite level, and that, as White women, they had some understanding of having to be one of the only women working in a predominantly male environment.

Ummm. . . No.

When the officer reached out to me, my advice was contrary to what she had received from those peers. I told her to leave the organization. There's no need to cast your pearls before swine.

Sometimes, well-intentioned advice or maybe even your pride and ego will keep you someplace past the expiration date. Leave when you can, before you are left with nothing.

Regardless of race, I would never advise you to stay where you are abused, victimized, tokenized, not wanted, or in any role that compromises your health.

I know that it can be easier said than done, but if you have the means to change teams, leave the company, switch classes, or enroll in a new school, do what you can to leave toxic places.

USING YOUR VOICE

After you've made time to practice the pause and regulate your emotions via journaling or verbally processing them with a therapist or a safe person, and you still feel unsettled, schedule a time to speak with the person who has mistreated you.

Before your conversation, ask yourself, "What do I want to come out of this?"

If it's an apology you're looking for, my question is, "If they don't apologize, what would be the point?"

If remorse and accountability are the outcomes you're striving for and what you're clinging to, you will be disappointed. You can still desire to have a positive resolution, but prepare for the possibility that things may not go as planned. It will not always be Kumbaya, and "We Are The World" will not start playing in the background.

Some people will just not say, "I'm sorry," or take accountability for their behavior, but that should not stop you from using your voice and self-advocating. Sometimes the most important person that needs to hear your voice is you. You need to listen to yourself and advocate for yourself. If that's your biggest takeaway, then be blessed.

> **Sometimes the most important person that needs to hear your voice is you.**

When you are ready to have the conversation, lead with facts, not feelings; you want to direct the discussion from an already regulated state. Although your emotions weren't acknowledged in the room when you faced their aggression, you can extend this empathy to yourself by holding space for your feelings. This way, when it's time for you to communicate with the other person, you can state how the experience made you feel without having the expression of those feelings take over the conversation.

You can say, "Yesterday, I felt threatened when you did this," or, "I felt disappointed that you didn't speak up because I view you not just as a colleague but as someone I respect." You're not yelling. You're not using curse words or being aggressive. You're simply articulating the effect of the microaggression.

You may wonder how you should handle people who say, "You're being too sensitive," when you call them out on their hurtful comments. Practice self-regulation, hold on to your viewpoint, and recognize that this can be a form of gaslighting. Since they chose to light that fire, you do not need to stay and get burned. Permit yourself to exit the conversation. When people use low emotional intelligence, don't match them. Just because they go low doesn't mean you have to go to the basement.

You can say something to the effect of, "It appears that we are not going to reach an understanding. My purpose was to let you know that what you said to me was unacceptable. I would hope that you would refrain from making those types of statements in the future."

You already know what I'm going to say next. Document that you had the conversation.

GET COMFORTABLE WITH OTHERS' DISCOMFORT

To my marginalized folk, specifically my Black readers, become comfortable with White discomfort.

I understand for my White readers that may be hard for some of you to read, but keep reading. Slow your amygdala down and become curious.

Your first thought may have been, "Farah, that's wrong! As a White person, if I told other White people to be comfortable with a Black person's discomfort, it would be considered racist."

You'd probably be right, but here's the difference. You've just read about code-switching, masking, microaggressions, and racial trauma in the previous chapters of this book, which explained how, historically, Black Americans have learned to create dysfunctional versions of themselves so they can have functional relationships in predominantly white spaces—meaning that Black people have been in a state of discomfort since the time of enslavement in the United States.

This discomfort has been their lived experience. Society has taught them to be uncomfortable with being Black, with their personhood, culture, and ethnicity. Black people can't change their race, but you can change your anti-Black ideology.

This White discomfort that I speak of comes up when racist behavior is called out. For my Black readers, part of your healing occurs when you learn to let your White peers wrestle with their racist ideology, rather than you wrestling with your Black identity. You must hold sacred space for your emotions and humanity to be valued, no longer dismissed for White comfort.

So, there is a difference. I'm hoping you understand what I'm saying. The creation of an environment where Black people are constantly in discomfort for the sake of White comfort is literally the society we live in today.

This is a self-care tool not just for Black people but for all persons who have been marginalized and othered. For your well-being, become comfortable with the discomfort of those in the majority whenever you call out someone's sexist, homophobic, ableist, or xenophobic ideology.

I've witnessed members of our society with Tourettes suffer in silence as they try to mask their tics to avoid making others uneasy. The same goes for our fellow humans with autism or ADHD who resist or hide their stimming. They do this to minimize being further othered by their peers.

Too many of us are unnecessarily living uncomfortably in our skin, so that we can appease others. We are taught to have shame for things often beyond our control.

In essence, we must all learn how to become more comfortable with discomfort.

Is this not how we change the narrative? We can increase our empathy and social awareness by asking ourselves, "Why is it okay for me to make someone feel 'othered' for my comfort?"

STOP MASKING

We understand that masking is a learned behavior. We have much unlearning to do to stop.

Even unmasking requires us to use our emotional intelligence. I don't recommend ripping off the mask, as unmasking can cause some distress. We must pace ourselves and measure our level of discomfort as we manage our emotions and responses to others as they react to our unmasking. Some will be more welcoming as you reintroduce yourself sans mask. Others might not like that you no longer fit into the box and identity in which they had put you.

Some people lose friends, familial relationships, and jobs when they unmask. May I give you a word of encouragement and insight? It could be that those who cannot accept your unmasked self lack the emotional intelligence to regulate their feelings regarding the change. People don't fear change; they fear loss.

Remember, you only have control over yourself. Learn to accept that you can't control people's reactions to that true self. Don't let their emotional dysregulation stop you from being genuine and comfortable in your skin.

When you are ready to unmask, first determine where it is safe to do so. Some families, workplaces, and schools are toxic and abusive, and the process of unmasking can result in more harm being caused. Remember, we learned in the previous chapters that the practice of masking started because there was a need to hide and protect oneself.

Once you find spaces where it is safe, begin practicing unmasking—this means learning how to be yourself even when it's scary. That can look like stimming in public or choosing to no longer hide an accent when speaking in certain circles.

Also, you can start talking more about unmasking. It never fails that, after every presentation I do on this topic, several attendees share that they had never heard of code-switching or masking. In a way, unmasking helps to bring awareness that can help others become more socially aware.

Hence, talking about masking and why you do it can help you unmask and control the narrative more. Explaining to others how you mask will give them a reference point from which they can better understand what is happening when you begin unmasking.

The more you can be your authentic self in various environments, the more energy you will have. It takes a lot of energy to be someone you are not. When you unmask, you will be able to bring your best self to the relationships that are important to you.

EQ-EXERCISE

Ask yourself these questions:

How do I mask?
Why do I mask?
In what ways am I being genuine?
In what ways am I being disingenuous?
How can I minimize these experiences of masking?
Who is safe to practice being my authentic self around?

GO TO THERAPY

There's a quote that reads, *"Heal, so we don't have another generation of trauma passing itself off as culture."*

As a therapist, it makes sense that I advocate going to therapy as part of your self-care toolkit.

There are so many benefits to therapy. It provides a space exclusively for you to process your emotions, receive feedback, be affirmed, and have someone walk with you as you heal and grow. Depending on your culture, there might be a more significant stigma around seeking the help of a mental health expert.

I understand that you might also be hesitant because you are uncertain about whether you will find a clinician that looks like you. At the end of this book, you will find a list of directories specific to the needs of many marginalized groups.

PART THREE:

FOR ALL(IES)

***

We started in black and white, then added some color. Now it's time to paint a picture: a picture showing how we can create a world where we all feel safe to be our best selves, because we decided to show up as our best selves for others by using the skill of emotional intelligence.

12

ALLYSHIP TO STEWARDSHIP

"I always wondered 'why somebody didn't do something about that.'
Then I realized I was somebody."

– Lily Tomlin

Allyship has become a popular word with a well-intended purpose. Here's the rub: although allyship is intended to be about inclusion, it can be unintentionally exclusive. It has us saying that we are aligned with a specific group. Today, it's the Asian community. Tomorrow, it's Black Lives Matter. Next, we're an ally to the LGBTQ+ community or those who are disabled.

I've watched people proclaim their allyship to certain groups based on whichever community seems to be "trending" on social media. The term is appealing, and many of us want to appear good. Therefore, we share an article, change our profile photo, or maybe even go to a rally. However, if you are only moved in the moment, is it really allyship? Allyship requires a long-term relationship, not a one-night stand.

There's also confusion about what allyship is. It's not only a noun but also an action verb. Even when it's used as a noun, it isn't a self-appointed identity or title. It's something you are recognized for by the evidence of your work and integrity of your character.

There must be receipts for your allyship.

Additionally, it isn't a linear goal; rather, it's something that can be incorporated into your lifestyle. Can you envision what allyship in action looks like for you? Take a moment to clarify your intention. Think about how you will feel when you start to activate your allyship.

I often get some version of this question: *"I want to be known as an ally; what can I do better?"* In essence, *"How can I be a good ally?"*

My question is, do you want to *be* a good ally or be *seen* as a good ally? Why does this distinction matter?

If you've learned anything from this book, I hope that it's to ask your-selves deeper questions. When you think of allyship, what comes to mind? What emotion does it evoke? Does the word seem appealing or aspirational? Are you confused about where to start? What does allyship look like for you?

You see, the title of ally doesn't necessarily mean anything. It's as hol-low as the phrase "I love you" if it is said without action. Although the sentiments of allyship may be pure, it's a limited view of what we all can be, that we can be allies with one another. Better yet, we can—and should—be better *stewards* of humanity. It isn't just about showing up for one group, but about showing up for all of humankind. We must be ambassadors of kindness in action.

Merriam-Webster defines stewardship as the conducting, supervising, or managing of something, especially the careful and responsible man-agement of something entrusted to one's care. When we look at the world, can we honestly say that we've stewarded it well? Whether it be nature or nurture, we've not done the best to manage this earth, its inhabitants, or its resources well.

We have created these hierarchies and committed horrible crimes against humanity. Instead of stewarding our interpersonal rela-tionships, we've been emotionally abusive, negligent, and careless.

However, this doesn't have to remain the narrative. We are all leaders, regardless of title. We all have something that is under our care. Our families, our friendships, our communities, and our places of work need us to be more responsible.

If we had managed our human relationships better, there wouldn't be a revolving door of hashtags: #BlackLivesMatter, #TransLivesMatter, #MeToo, or an "I Stand With (fill in the blank). We have failed to walk in true empathy with one another. It may be due to our own pain and trauma, which has left us apathetic.

These hashtags were created because our societies are overwhelmed with bystanders. Throughout past and present history, we have watched people be complicit in hatred, discrimination, and bigotry by remaining silent or through their inaction. We have accepted harassment as commonplace and enabled abusers by describing their behavior as commonplace.

We've heard the saying, "boys will be boys." What does that even mean? We've already discussed society's emotional narrative around masculinity and how it has not served us well. There are too many women who know other women that have been raped, yet there are men who state that they don't know any rapists. I'm sorry, but that math ain't mathing.

I get it. It seems daunting to unravel major systems of oppression. You are up against centuries of entrenched beliefs and structures, and simply desiring society to be different is not enough. If it feels overwhelming for you, imagine what it feels like to be the ones that are mistreated. Especially those who live within multiple intersectionalities of marginalization.

However, this work isn't a solo mission. It's been said that many hands make light work. The problem is that there are too many idle hands, or hands that, clothed in self-righteousness, clumsily create more problems.

By reading this book, you are now more knowledgeable of the systemic inequities that may cause people to not show up as their authentic selves. How do you help to create psychologically safe spaces? How do you elevate your emotional intelligence to prevent underrepresented people from feeling the need to mask? You must become both socially- and self-aware so that you can steward your sphere of influence.

Showing up as an ally doesn't require a cape or an "A" on your chest. A musical score won't play when you enter a room, sign a petition, or join a protest. It isn't loud. It does not boast. Allyship can be subtle, but never covert.

WHY THIS MATTERS

When we recognize that allyship, stewardship, partnership—or whatever new term we come up with to simply describe being humane—isn't about performative actions, but is evidence of our values, we will move differently in the world. Let's stop looking for gold stars, but seek to find the light within ourselves and others.

-EQ REVIEW-

- If we aren't careful, allyship can be exclusionary when we choose to support only one underrepresented group and ignore or deny others.

- Allyship is a verb that requires consistent action and relationship with others.

- Allyship is not self-appointing and should not be performative.

- Our goal is to be better *stewards* of humanity so we can show up for *all* humankind, not just one group.

- We have not stewarded our world well, which has damaged both earth and its inhabitants.

- Allyship is not a solo mission, it is done collectively.

13

PRIVILEGE

*"The most dangerous advantage of privilege is the power
of the privileged to deny its existence."*

— *Colton Poore*

"Can we use another word? Perhaps blessed?"

This is what someone asked me during our conversation about the
word *privilege*. They readily admitted that the word made them uneasy.
My response to their suggestion was, "If I am blessed with sight at
birth, what does that mean for someone who wasn't?"

Immediately, the other person recognized that the euphemism was
inadequate and potentially harmful.

Now let me ask you, when you hear the word "privilege," what comes
up for you? Does it prickle you? Are you already preparing your
defense about how you are not privileged? Let's exercise the three A's.
Beginning with awareness, can you name the emotion that you feel
when you think of the word privilege? Allow yourself to experience
the feeling without judgment.

Next, it's time to assess, "What is it about this word that makes you
feel this way?"

This may be a bit challenging. You might have to peel a few layers away from the onion. It's okay; remember, no judgment here. If you find that anger is the emotion that comes up for you, clarify the story behind the feeling. Are you able to identify your narrative or belief around the word and where it came from? If not, that's alright. We can unpack and address this together.

Merriam-Webster defines privilege as a right, immunity, or benefit enjoyed by a particular person or a restricted group of people beyond the advantages of most.

A common misconception is that privilege solely equates to status or wealth; this is not the case. Wealth most certainly is a privilege, but that isn't the only area of privilege that exists. Other examples of privilege can be height, weight, skin color, education, age, physical ability, or health.

It isn't necessarily something of which to be proud or ashamed. It simply is what it is.

Privilege can be something you are born with, or something acquired. It isn't necessarily something of which to be proud or ashamed. It simply is what it is. We must also recognize that our privileges aren't always permanent. We can have wealth today and lose it tomorrow. We can be in good health today and become ill tomorrow, or, due to illness or an accident, we can become disabled.

It's important to understand that privilege is about what rights and advantages you have that another person or group may not have, and what you do with those rights and advantages. It can be helpful to look at our areas of privilege as resources that can be used for good.

For instance, at the grocery store, those items on the top shelf can be difficult to get to when you're a person of a particular height. It's always a welcoming relief when a tall person sees your predicament and pulls down the very item that you couldn't reach. However, while your height may limit you from reaching something that's up high, your age or lack of a physical disability provides you the privilege to bend down to grab something low that an elderly or physically disabled person can't easily reach down to get. These are basic examples of privilege, but they are privileges, nonetheless.

We develop emotional responses to things based on the ways words have been presented to us. In recent years, the word "privilege" has not stood alone but has been accompanied by the word "White." When you put these two words together, whew, it ruffles some feathers. It's interesting what ends up feeling like a 4-letter cuss word. Tell someone they are privileged and suddenly defenses, deflection, and denial come up. Part of this is due to a lack of critical thinking on their part in their rush to protect themselves.

"What are you trying to say? That I didn't earn this? I work hard. I'm a smart person!'"

According to Kelley Bonner, we all have levels of privilege, yet there's a kind of fragility that comes with it that puts us in a defensive position. When privilege is highlighted, no one is saying that you are not smart, or hard working, or that things haven't been difficult for you. You are simply being asked not to deny the advantages that the privileges you have afford you.

Bonner says that it's our ego that gets the best of us. We continuously want to prove that we're not a bad person—there's a deep-seated desire in us to be seen as good and moral people. It's this psychology of self that makes us rattled at the idea that we could have an unfair advantage over someone else or a benefit due to something as uncontrollable as our skin color.

How about this: have you ever thought about how the hand you write with can be considered a privilege? Left-handed people make up approximately ten percent of the western population. To be left-handed is to be unique, but it places one in the minority. When we consider the historical narratives surrounding handedness, left-handed people have been considered unlucky, negative, or even evil by the right-handed majority.

In many languages, the word for the direction "right" also means "correct" or "proper." In French, *gauche* means both "left" and "awkward" or "clumsy," while *droit(e)* means both "right" and "straight." To have "two left feet" is to describe a poor dancer and a "left-handed compliment" is one that has two meanings, one of which is unflattering to the recipient.

Even into the 20th century, left-handed children were beaten by school teachers for writing with their left hand. My own father shared that he only writes with his right hand because, as a child, his teachers would tap him with a ruler whenever he used his left hand to write as a reminder to use his right hand instead. If all of this has taken place towards those who are left-handed, imagine what it's been like for those who have been systemically excluded due to their race, gender, or sexual orientation?

In Part One, we talked about the different barriers that make it difficult for us to practice our emotional intelligence, and one of them was being self-centered. This can cause us to have an antagonistic disposition and a strong belief that we've had a tough life, had real struggles, and that we're inarguably good people. Coupled with our society touting that our outcomes are due to meritocracy, the notion that we have unearned advantages challenges that. We end up making everything about ourselves and we tell the story we want to tell, absent of the truth of privilege, because that makes us feel better.

Privilege doesn't necessarily equate to an easier life; it means that your life isn't made harder due to certain attributes that are often discriminated against.

It's true that we all face hardships. However, these hardships do not negate the presence of privilege.

Privilege doesn't necessarily equate to an easier life; it means that your life isn't made harder due to certain attributes that are often discriminated against.

However, if we move in the spirit of denial, we actively choose to negate the reality of our privilege. It isn't that you are unable to see the truth, but more so that you refuse to admit the truth that privilege exists.

If this is your default response, you are not practicing emotional intelligence. You cannot say that you are aware, yet deny the natural and social constructs of privilege. How can you effectively address the real issues and damages that have been caused by said privilege if you fail to address racism and the hierarchy created from it? Can we do the same with patriarchy and sexism? Do we dismiss the painful history of these systems simply to appease our psyche?

The 1999 film The Matrix depicts a dystopian society in which humanity is unknowingly trapped inside a simulated reality. There is an option to leave the Matrix if one chooses the red pill over the blue pill. Ingesting the red pill would allow one to learn potentially life-changing truths through seeing the previously hidden reality. This pill represents reasoning, critical thinking, and knowing the real truth.

On the contrary, the blue pill allows you to stay in a state of simple, uncritical belief. To remain in contented ignorance and emotional decision making.

If we try to play the game of cognitive dissonance and choose to live in *The Matrix*, we build a reality not based on truth. To have emotional intelligence is to be aware of what the real problem is. The problem isn't White people, it's White supremacy and racism. The problem isn't men, but patriarchy and sexism. The problem isn't heterosexuality, it's homophobia. The problem isn't non-disabled people, it's ableism.

> **When we fail to see something for what it is, we become inactive. Worse yet, we become complicit.**

When we fail to see something for what it is, we become inactive. Worse yet, we become complicit.

Raising our awareness minimizes our tendency to become defensive or idle in working together to dismantle these systems. Remember, privilege isn't something about which to feel guilty. It's a resource that can be used for the greater good.

EQ-Tip

A quick note. When you acknowledge the truth of these constructs, be cautious not to distance yourself from the privileges these constructs provide you, nor the oppression that they cause in order to forsake your ego's discomfort—to say, "I'm not like them!"

Gina, a Black woman, was asked to testify in a congressional hearing as a subject matter expert for an agency on sexual harassment and sexual violence in the workplace. She prepared for the whole thing and wrote the testimony. When she sent it to the Department of Commerce to get cleared, it got shot down by the Heads of Commerce because they didn't like two phrases she had in the testimony. Therefore, they refused to let her testify and made the decision to have a White man testify in her place.

Although Gina couldn't testify, she was tasked with preparing this White man for the hearing. The irony is that he had to use her words for the testimony. For a total of 15 hours she had to work with him because he wasn't the subject matter expert, she was. During their time together, he had told her, "I want you to know that I'm not unaware that the only reason I was asked to do this, is because I'm a White man."

On the day of the hearing, after reading her testimony, he says, "I want to be clear that the subject matter expert on this is Gina." He then stated, "She's who we leaned on for all this information and it's her leadership that got us to where we are today. We would not be here without her."

As he walked out of that congressional hearing, he recognized that this Black woman was overqualified in her current role. He asked, "Who do I need to speak to, to make you a director?"

He sent an email to HR, who had been blocking Gina's advancement. He advocated for her promotion and she got it. This man understood how his race and gender gave him advantages that weren't based solely on merit. He didn't refuse them. He didn't feel shame or guilt that he had them. Instead, he used his privilege to be of service to her. He stewarded what was given to him and allocated his resources to the one who was denied them.

Be aware that it is even a privilege to have stayed in ignorance of the plight of racially and ethnically marginalized people. I recall when a leader from a Fortune 100 company stated during a panel discussion how, since the summer of 2020, she began to gain a greater understanding of what her Black colleagues had been dealing with for years.

"I had no idea about the situations that they were going through every day." Her comment wasn't the first time I had heard this. Similar sentiments have been shared since the murder of George Floyd and as diversity, equity, and inclusion have become go-to points of discussion.

Her being unaware of the racial trauma her colleagues experienced in and out of the workplace was a privilege. Her sudden awakening is a grim reminder to her Black colleagues that they were unseen and unheard prior to Floyd's murder.

Trust me, Black people don't feel any comfort when you say, "I didn't know it was this bad." Telling a Black person that you didn't realize the level of disrespect and racial bias that occurred towards them in the workplace isn't affirming. It's confirming that you weren't socially aware and didn't take the time to see their challenges.

There are White parents who express concern about discussing racism and race with their children. Their belief is that their child is too young to be burdened with these topics, yet Black children are never too young to experience racism.

There's a famous photograph of Ruby Bridges being escorted out of William Frantz Elementary School in Louisiana. At the tender age of six, she was the first African American child to desegregate the all-White school in 1959.

Ruby and her mother had to be escorted by four federal marshals to school every day that year for her safety. She had to walk past crowds of adults and children hurling slurs at her. Frighteningly, one woman even held a Black baby doll in a coffin.

Angry White parents pulled their children from the school, and only one teacher was willing to accept Ruby. She ate lunch alone and some-times played with her teacher at recess. For an entire year, she was in a class of one.

Can you imagine what that was like for her day in and day out? Or for the countless other persons who were the first to desegregate an all-White school, department, board, or organization? To be unaware of what they endured daily is a costly privilege to have. It robs you and others of the gift of empathy and motivation to act.

I'd like for us to throw away this internal belief that privilege is a bad thing and something from which we must distance ourselves, or that it's something we should reject simply because it leaves us feeling "some type of way." What's bad is when privilege goes unchecked or is denied. The lack of awareness, both self and social, along with a lack of regulating oneself when someone highlights your privilege, doesn't foster any kind of resolve. To acknowledge your privilege is not for you to feel shame, but to elevate your self- and social awareness so that you may use the power of your privilege for good.

In the words of Voltaire, or Peter Parker's Uncle Ben in Spiderman (I'm not judging your choice of philosophers), "with great power comes great responsibility."

I know some of you don't like the fact that I've come down your street and may have stepped on some toes. I sincerely am doing so in love to help move you in the direction where we all care about the lived experiences of others.

So, are you still hung up on the word "privilege," or are you beginning to recognize how a word can be hijacked and turned into something more than what it is simply due to the narrative that one places on it? What privileges have you been able to identify for yourself? See if you can recognize how they can be used to serve another and how they show up in your life. If feelings of resistance return, and they will, don't fret: you know what to do now.

WHY THIS MATTERS

We all have privileges. Some of us have more privileges than others. These advantages do not make us better than or less than someone else. The diversity in our privilege can be beneficial, allowing us to help those in need. This means that there are moments when our privilege will benefit someone else, and there are times when their privilege benefits us. Removing the stigma around privilege can help us become more charitable and collaborative instead of cruel and combative.

Now that you are more self-aware of your privilege, let's increase your social awareness to help you identify how you can better read the room.

-EQ REVIEW-

- We all have privilege.

- Privilege is not a bad word.

- Not all privileges are permanent.

- To deny privilege is to live outside of reality.

- It's a privilege to be unaware of someone else's life experiences.

- Our privileges are to be used in service of others.

14

READ THE ROOM

"With awareness comes responsibility and choice."

— Amanda Linhout

There are two popular expressions that have to do with elephants. One is "the elephant in the room," a metaphor related to an obvious problem that people avoid discussing or acknowledging.

The other is an African Proverb that reminds us that "there's only one way to eat an elephant, and that's one bite at a time."

I think about these expressions when I consider how we address the topics of inequality and allyship.

Many of us are either scared of or apprehensive with addressing the elephant in the room. Heck, there are some who aren't even aware that there's an elephant to begin with! In dismantling oppressive systems, we individually and collectively struggle with breaking the problems down because our eyes are too big for our stomachs.

As much as I'd like these systems to fall in one big swoop, it's unrealistic. They're just too big. We end up biting off way more than we can chew, which is extremely difficult and tiring, especially when what we've eaten is hard to digest. The way to rightly identify the elephant in the room and to properly "eat" it is with emotional intelligence.

Before we can even sink our teeth into it, we must first acknowledge that there's a problem. Social awareness allows us to not only know that there's an elephant, but it also challenges us to call out where it is, identify its size, and recognize what it is doing in the room. This is us acknowledging that -isms exist, and that they negatively impact the environment and people emotionally, mentally, and physically.

Remember the example about being left-handed? Well, when I was growing up, most classrooms had the desk attached to the chair. The majority of these desks were built for right-handed students. As a right-handed individual, when I entered the room, I only thought about where and who I would sit next to. I never once questioned whether the actual function of the desk was made with me in mind. Even the pencil sharpener on the wall, with its handle on the right, was designed for me.

For those of you who are left-handed, you may already know where I'm going with this. If you were a lefty, you often had to check whether there was a desk for you. You had to scan the room to see where you belonged.

Because it wasn't my lived experience, I was oblivious to what was lacking in the room because I was a part of the majority. However, these desks, pencil sharpeners, scissors, and even our spiral notebooks were reminders to those who were left-handed that they were in the minority and their needs were, and for the most part, still are, an afterthought.

When the rooms are designed with you in mind, you aren't even aware of what is lacking.

It wasn't until my younger sister, who's a "lefty," brought to my attention how she navigated spaces that were predominantly for right-handed individuals, that I started to pay more attention. I noticed the advantages and disadvantages of being left-handed in a predominantly right-handed world. When the rooms are designed with you in mind, you aren't even aware of what is lacking. That's a privilege.

Until cancer hit your home, did you really care about cancer research?

Until you had a child with unique needs, were you concerned about inclusivity?

Until you knew someone with paraplegia, did you notice the lack of accessible spaces?

"It wasn't until after my dad's accident and he ended up being in a wheelchair that I became more aware of my surroundings," is what one LinkedIn user shared with me. "I saw how he would struggle and no one cared to help."

Let's imagine for a moment that you had a physical disability. Would your home or your workplace be easy to maneuver through? Are the entrances accessible? If you live someplace where it snows or rains often, how would that impact you?

Much of the struggle around diversity, equity, and inclusion is that people have difficulty empathizing with something that is not their lived experience. Until situations personally affect you or someone close to you, you may easily overlook and not intentionally make accommodations or be aware of inequities.

Things don't become dear to us until they become near to us.

In other words, things don't become dear to us until they become near to us.

Can you recall a moment that brought some awareness to not only someone else's lived experience but also highlighted your privilege? Broadening and diversifying your network and community helps to expand your lens. Doing so helps to increase empathy and ideally moves your allyship into action.

You address the elephant by reading the room, recognizing who's in it and who isn't. For those who are there, I ask you to consider: what are those in the room doing, and how are they being treated? What do they have access to, and what barriers are in place for some and not for others? Whose suggestions get listened to, and who gets ignored?

Look around and see how the elephant is taking up space. Pay attention to which group gets rewarded for the same behavior that gets another group punished. Who gets promoted, and who doesn't? Who's made to feel uncomfortable, and who is at ease?

Part of allyship work is to intentionally check your surroundings. It is to actively draw nearer to other people's experiences so that you can increase your social awareness. If you are only engaging and walking through life with people who look just like you, who think just like you, and who have the same experience as you, this can become problematic. I've seen this issue present itself in the professional arena.

"What in the White people parade is this?!" Exclaimed one of my colleagues. I had shared with her the speaker list for an upcoming conference and, as a White woman, she was shocked that there weren't any identifiable people of color on the roster.

Organizations and boards plan events that they are excited to promote, then are surprised by the backlash because everyone on their panel is all White or all men and say, "Oh no! How did this happen?"

I can tell you how it happened. It was because they did not choose to be intentional about creating a diverse community. Worse yet, when it's brought to their attention, they try to quickly remedy it by tokenizing someone. Please don't do that. Adding a Black person or a woman at the last minute, using someone as a band-aid, just adds insult to injury.

Tokenism is the practice of making a symbolic effort or gesture to be inclusive to members of systemically excluded groups in order to give the appearance of equality. This is often done to prevent criticism by showing that what you are doing is what is expected or seen as fair.

I, personally, had the unfortunate and painful experience of being tokenized. While I was sharing the situation with a dear friend of mine, she admitted that, as a White woman, she missed what was occurring to me. She stated how when she saw the advertisement of the event, her first thought was, "Wow! Look at my friend!"

On the contrary, all my Black friends saw something suspicious, and it was glaring to them. Their suspicion was valid. When I spoke with the organizer after the event, I asked why my image was used on their marketing material as one of their keynote speakers, when in previous drafts, I had not been.

You see, I wasn't a keynote speaker or even on a panel. My contribution was minimal—I was asked to provide a short pre-recorded video. Two White women were asked to provide the same thing. Surprisingly, the photos of those two women weren't bumped up and added to the list.

The organizer admitted that the feedback they had received during the initial marketing was that their event lacked diversity—so they added me. I wonder what made me so special?

I called them out on not only their tokenism but how the choice to use only me and not the other two women who provided the same level of service to the event was inequitable.

An argument could be made that it was free exposure. Take a second and reflect on that. Is this the kind of exposure that you would want for yourself? Would you want to be highlighted, not because of your knowledge, credentials, or expertise, but because of your race, gender, or disability?

Tokenism isn't a favor.

Tokenism isn't a favor. No one wants to be a check in a box.

These missteps occur when we neglect to implement emotional intelligence in the prep work. Then, when given a moment of awareness, we try to troubleshoot, and we stumble there as well, because we fail to take responsibility for our actions.

If you've tokenized someone in the past, use your emotional intelligence to self-regulate and hold yourself accountable. Do the work so that you don't become a repeat offender. Don't continue to talk to the same circle of people expecting a different result. That's the definition of insanity.

Once you've been called out, recognize that you can do something about it and do not be defensive. Becoming defensive isn't taking accountability. Take what you've learned, practice the pause, and identify what emotions are being exposed.

Social awareness also teaches us to assess a room before we jump into a conversation. It helps us to be mindful of our words. However, privilege can lower your awareness so that you don't even bother to read the room—you subconsciously feel that you *own* the room.

Being in the majority can cause some to act like everything is theirs and that they have the right to say and do what they want. Privilege and unchecked biases are usually contributors to these microaggressions when they occur.

Early in my husband's career, he attended an event at a racetrack as part of a company outing. The owner of a firm that partnered with his company was hosting the event and the owner was an older White man in his seventies.

"I didn't know that Black people were allowed at racetracks," is what he said to my husband.

At first, my husband thought maybe this gentleman was joking, but then he repeated himself, "I don't believe that Black people are allowed here."

My husband nervously laughed it off, unsure of what to say, afraid to do anything that might anger the client and possibly get him fired. As a Black man in his early twenties, he felt clueless as to how to respond.

"That was inappropriate. This is one of our team members, and he's getting ready to come in with us." This is what my husband's boss said to the client. He had overheard the exchange and stepped in.

He was firm, and my husband could tell by the look on his face that his boss was deeply disturbed and upset. I'm not sure if he knew what thoughts and emotions my husband had, but he was clearly aware of the big racist elephant in the room, and he didn't wait for the moment to pass to privately acknowledge and apologize for the racism my husband encountered. He didn't wait to see how his Black employee would react. He knew for himself that what was said, what was happening, was unacceptable, hateful, and disrespectful behavior that he would not condone in his presence.

In this situation, we see two White men interact with the room differently. One believed he owned the room and could decide who was allowed in it based on his racist beliefs and mindset. His privilege and way of thinking gave him permission to lower all the levels of emotional intelligence. He wasn't empathetic or kind and he didn't care how his words landed on my husband—showing low self- and social awareness. He didn't regulate his emotions, and his relationship management skills were non-existent.

Then we have my husband's boss, another White man with similar privilege, who read the room very differently. He empathized with my husband and knew that what was said to him was unkind. He was able to self-regulate his emotions so that he could effectively communicate his disapproval and what he was unwilling to tolerate. He was socially and self-aware enough to know that he was in the position to say something and be an upstander in the face of hate.

Allies can help take some of the burdens from the people facing aggression from others by using their voices. If you are in the room and something is stated by a friend, a colleague, or by a leader that is unacceptable, whether well-intended or not, it's an opportunity for a teachable moment. Don't wait for those on the receiving end of injustice to speak up.

While identifying the elephant in the room, we are also aware of who we are in respect to the elephant and the other people in the room. We're aware of how we are landing on those people. We can be insensitive based on our inability to see that elephant. Removing our blinders can help to increase our compassion for others, acknowledge their needs, and decrease being reckless with our words and actions.

In becoming more emotionally intelligent, we can begin recognizing that we're all sharing the room and that there are obstacles in the room that we hadn't seen before. Obstacles that don't affect us but limit freedoms of and access for others. Elevating our EQ helps us to not avoid addressing the elephant and guides us when we have difficult conversations.

Not only that, our EQ helps us to anticipate that elephant. This anticipation helps us to better prepare physically and psychologically safe spaces. For instance, when planning that great event, build out your list of speakers who are diverse in advance, so you don't leave anyone feeling like they are the only chocolate chip in the cookie. As an interior designer, think beyond just creating a wheelchair-accessible bathroom—make sure that the entire layout of a room is easy to navigate from entrance to exit.

That's the critical moment, that moment of awareness. There's no sin in not knowing that there should have been a ramp or there should have been left-handed desks. That's the problem people get caught up on. It's not like we're saying you're a bad person because you didn't know, but once you do know, what are you doing to help?

IDENTIFY BLIND SPOTS

When you are learning to drive a car, you are instructed to not only use your side mirrors but also to turn your head in case you missed a car in your blind spot when changing lanes. Regardless of the car's design, nearly all vehicles have at least one blind spot, and the only way that you can circumvent this blind spot is by moving from the traditional driving position.

You have to take your eyes off the road in front of you, but it's the only way for you to observe the activity surrounding you. These blind spots are dangerous because they prevent you from noticing what's around you that could cause harm.

We must be aware of our blind spots as we drive down the highway of life and understand that we are sharing the road with others. If we don't take a moment to look and see what's happening around us, we will miss out. We should not assume that all is well and that no one is in harm's way.

Many of us have blind spots that hinder us from showing up well for others. We miss microaggressions because we are looking for overt acts of bias and discrimination. Microaggressions can be very covert. Don't assume that acts of oppression and marginalization happen only in obvious ways. It's important to genuinely get to know more diverse people to understand their experiences.

When expanding your circle, you will not only gain a better perspective, but will also be challenged to think critically and not accept things at face value, because you just might be missing something—something hurtful.

When you build your community, engage from an organic and genuine level. Don't try to create relationships just because it seems like the right thing to do. Disingenuous relationships create a false sense of solidarity and further erode trust. Be authentic and intentional.

Including more people from various backgrounds helps to provide perspectives and decrease blind spots.

We must continue to grow in awareness to see what's out of our line of sight. Otherwise, we end up missing so much. Our increased social awareness helps us recognize that others are in the room and ensure they have what they need to succeed so that everyone has an equitable experience.

Also, recognize that just because someone is a member of a group, that doesn't mean that they will have the same experiences as others within that group. For example, you can't group all women's experiences together as being one and the same. White women's experiences aren't the same as Black women's, or Black women's experiences and those of Asian women. Even within a set racialized group, there are unique experiences.

Don't generalize from limited, second-hand stories. Have intentional and authentic conversations with many so you can become more attuned to their unique experiences and intersectional identities.

FEEDBACK

Earlier, I stated that you can't have self-awareness absent of feedback. It is this feedback that helps to reinforce or discourage certain behavior. Feedback can help minimize blind spots and elevate awareness.

For example, when you're on the receiving end of someone's allyship, you provide them feedback. Not as a reward, but as fuel, to encourage that behavior so they can be a good model for others.

Recall the example of Gina, the Black woman who was asked to testify at a congressional hearing but ended up being replaced by a White man. At the end of his testimony, not only did he acknowledge her work, but he also advocated for her to be promoted. In return, she

effectively communicated her appreciation and stated how she benefited from him truly seeing her.

She wasn't effusive, nor did she self-deprecate and say, "If it wasn't for
you, where would I have been?"

No, she knew that she deserved the promotion, but she also knew that
she needed someone to champion her in that process because of the
discrimination she had faced. By giving him context to her gratitude,
she provided the feedback needed to help him be more self-aware and
socially aware so that he'd continue to show up as an ally in future
situations.

We need to affirm this behavior in an authentic way. Not to placate or
pacify someone's ego, but to acknowledge that many people won't take
the risk that they did. When someone's allyship impacts your life, you
lose nothing by telling them that. What you gain is someone who will
continue to do the good work.

There's a line that we must toe in not becoming adversarial with people in allyship roles, yet not going overboard with making them the
focus in their allyship. We want to highlight what was done and have
them continue to learn and apply it.

It is similar to an athlete who is training for an event. You don't con-
gratulate them after they've run one mile. You cheer them on so that
they can keep building endurance and keep going.

Allyship is a constant reinforcement: action and reinforcement, then
practice and reinforcement. Unfortunately, we don't always allow people the space to practice and fail. We also don't provide reinforcement
when they get it right.

WHY THIS MATTERS

Social awareness is not only needed to help us be empathetic with one another, but it helps us to identify and anticipate the needs of others. In doing so, we can provide accommodations, advocacy, and access to those who need it. When we are socially aware, fewer deficiencies are present because each person is offering what is needed on behalf of others.

For effective change to occur, we need to know what works and then be consistent with it. However, for us to know what action in our allyship is productive, we need feedback from others. If we want to keep our allyship light burning, it is imperative that we not only seek feedback from others but that we provide feedback to others.

In the next chapter, we will learn additional tools that will help us not to diminish the flame.

-EQ REVIEW-

- Social awareness allows us to not only know that there's an elephant in the room, but it also challenges us to call out where it is, identify its size, and recognize what it is doing in that room.

- You address the elephant by reading the room, by recognizing who's in it, and who isn't.

- The work of dismantling systems and barriers is daunting and requires us to not tackle it all at once.

- The struggle around diversity, equity, and inclusion is that people have difficulty empathizing with something that is not their lived experience. Things don't become dear to us until they are near to us.

- Allies can help take some of the burdens off of the people who are being aggressed by using their voice.

- Being a part of a more diverse community, along with getting feedback from trusted individuals, can help you to identify blind spots.

- We need to affirm someone's allyship in an authentic way, not to placate or pacify their ego but to reinforce behavior by providing feedback.

15

ONE BITE AT A TIME

*"The victims of oppression don't need our spasms of passion,
but our long obedience in the same direction."*

– Gary Haugen

If you've ever had to care for a family member who was ill, aging, or had a physical disability, although you love them, taking care of them can be stressful, even if you have help. To avoid extreme exhaustion, you must also take care of yourself while supporting your loved ones. To protect yourself, you must learn self-care strategies.

It is the same with our allyship. We may not realize that it requires us to practice emotionally intelligent self-care. In Chapter 12, we discussed the importance of using emotional intelligence as part of your self-care practice if you are part of a historically marginalized group. We must also use this skill set in our advocacy and allyship, otherwise, we can lose steam, become complacent, and experience burnout.

You might be thinking: how in the world can I experience burnout as a result of showing up for others and living out my values? Well, friend, being able to show up for others, to hold space, and put your allyship into action takes work. Are you familiar with the term *compassion fatigue*? It's a term that describes the emotional, physical, and psychological impact of helping others, and it causes exhaustion and reduces our ability to empathize.

In my line of work, I advocate for the well-being of my clients. I help them to use their voice and process pain, and I come alongside them as they evolve into becoming the best, healed version of themselves. To do my job effectively, I have to be self-aware and self-regulate so that I don't pull focus away from my client during their sessions. I must minimize countertransference, which occurs when a therapist transfers their emotions to their clients.

Of course, I'm aware that you all aren't therapists. However, there are aspects of the therapeutic relationship that align with allyship. Listening, championing, advocating, de-centering oneself, and affirming are some of the actions that are part of allying with others. If we aren't mindful, we can end up tiring out in this act of service. We can begin experiencing compassion fatigue and burnout.

Burnout is defined as a state of emotional, physical, and psychological exhaustion caused by excessive and chronic stress. It's quite common, especially when it involves emotionally and psychologically heavy work.

There's often the misconception that burnout is caused because we are stressed out doing work we dislike. On the contrary, we can experience burnout while doing the very thing we enjoy and are passionate about if we aren't careful to implement boundaries and practice self-care.

I've seen many therapists get burned out because they didn't put proper boundaries in place, especially during the Covid-19 pandemic. There was such a desire to help that clinicians filled their calendars up in hopes of providing services for those who were struggling. In doing so, they ended up neglecting to care for themselves as they, too, were managing through the trauma of the pandemic.

When we show up as allies, we need to know that there are levels to this. Our allyship will not look the same. How I steward my privilege may not be the same way you steward yours. For some of you, your allyship may consist of activism, and, with that activism, there are various degrees of involvement.

There is short-term and low-risk activism, such as calling your senator or attending a non-violent protest, to long-term and high-risk activism, which can be challenging and more dangerous. Even if you're not on the physical front lines of a protest, you may find that your allyship requires you to take risks at work and with your family and friends.

According to one study, 87% of peace activists quit activism within six years of getting involved because they get burned out. For marginalized activists, burnout is even more prevalent, not only due to the stresses of activism but also from dealing with the everyday acts of racism and oppression. Similarly, there's high turnover for DEI practitioners because, as I stated before, it is hard to be both the advocate and the abused.

Inequities, discrimination, racism, sexism, and bias aren't necessarily fun topics to discuss. They're not always energizing. These topics are heavy, especially if you are on the receiving end. Nevertheless, these are necessary conversations that cause us to lean into our discomfort in acknowledging -isms and their historical systemic effects.

It isn't comfortable. It can be traumatic. Therefore, I encourage all who are determined to align with those who've been historically marginalized and disenfranchised to pace yourselves.

Allyship isn't a sprint; it's not even a marathon, because there isn't a finish line. We are ever evolving, and, with this evolution, we can choose to keep getting better or stay in our comfort zone. It's a privilege to fade away from doing the good work of allyship. It's understandable that you may become overwhelmed by new information and that your empathy threshold may become limited. However, if this work is aligned with your values, I know you will keep pushing forward.

As much as I would like to rid the world of these social cancers with a snap of my fingers like Thanos in Marvel's *Avengers: Infinity War*, these suckers aren't going to go away quickly. These issues—these systems—were created and are upheld by people every day. For things to change, that requires people to change. That's not an easy feat.

Change frightens us because we fear what we may lose. It requires us to think, feel, and do things differently. However, when we use our emotional intelligence, it allows us to be more adaptable and flexible. We're able to better self-regulate and "walk our dog" in a way that helps us be more resilient and reduce our need to kick our survival mode into high gear.

> **Change frightens us because we fear what we may lose.**

You can tell, collectively, that we don't do well with change. Just look at how we reacted to the Covid-19 pandemic! We watched people ignore health guidelines and protocols because they were inconvenienced by the changes the coronavirus brought to their doorstep. Cognitive dissonance was on full display as people continued to go to parties, travel, and complain about their loss of freedom because they didn't know how to practice the pause and self-regulate.

Our resistance to change can end up bringing out the worst in us. The fight-flight-or-freeze response lowers our emotional intelligence and ability to empathize. We are unable to rationally and reasonably respond to the change. How many times did you hear, "I wish we could just get back to normal?" or "I'm ready for this to be over!" Unfortunately, the normal that we once knew will never fully return. We must learn to move forward to the next normal.

Similarly, with diversity, equity, inclusion, and anti-racism being promoted, we see many people bucking back. There's new language, particularly buzzwords like: microaggressions, privilege, intersectionality, neurodiversity, allyship, patriarchy, cisgender, and others that leave some feeling lost, incompetent, and fearful. For some of us, we are hyper-socially aware, and we endure much frustration with those who seem to be walking around in a state of blissful ignorance.

There's this expectation that some people should be where we want them to be—which is a lot further along. We first must acknowledge where they are so that we can meet them there and take them to where we want them to go.

It's been extremely tiring living with racism, misogyny, homophobia, and the like, and it can be equally as tiring trying to move people and the needle towards progressive change. This is why we need to give each other grace as we move forward, because these issues are loaded and this is emotionally heavy stuff that weighs on us.

PACE YOURSELF

When you do any type of physical training, you must start small, or you can hurt yourself. No one starts weight training with 150-pound weights, or runs ten miles in preparation for a marathon on the first day. No, you might start out with a five-pound weight, or try to run half a mile. This is how you strengthen muscle and build endurance. It's the same with serving your fellow humans. You can't do it all, and you most certainly can't do it all at once. Remember the elephant? One bite at a time.

In claiming the identity of an ally, you might find yourself wanting to separate yourself from having any affiliation with "the oppressors." No one wants to feel like they are on the wrong side of history. Who wants to be connected to systems that have caused great evil and distress? There's fear of being lumped in with all White people, all men, or all Christians.

Let's not forget that the war isn't against people, it's against systems.

Let's not forget that the war isn't against people, it's against systems.

At the same time, as you become more aware of your privilege, you may start to feel powerless to do anything about it. If this occurs, identify the beliefs and or barriers that stand in the way of you being an active ally. Practice using your self-awareness to call out those limiting beliefs, such as: *I lack the confidence; I feel powerless; this isn't my fault; I don't think that I'm part of the problem.*

All of these thoughts can become excuses for inaction. Reflect on what allyship means and looks like for you. How you show up in your allyship work will not necessarily look like the next person's, and that's okay. You determine what that "authentically" looks like for you.

Use your discernment and your self-awareness to determine your bandwidth. You can't be at all the protests. You can't watch all the documentaries in one sitting. You can't read all the books. Attempting to do so will leave you like many activists and DEI advocates: ignited by the truth, but your flame will quickly burn out due to a lack of self-care.

The more your eyes see and the more truth you digest, you may run the risk of becoming hardened or sick. Don't consume it all too quickly. You can still experience vicarious or secondary trauma even if you do not identify with the traumatized group.

Focus your allyship on creating evidence-based tactics that will drive small wins within your sphere of influence and create opportunities to interact through networking, mentoring, and professional development events.

SET BOUNDARIES

Why do we argue with strangers on social media platforms? Like, *seriously*? More often than not, it is a waste of our time. Mark Twain said it best: "Never argue with a fool, onlookers may not be able to tell the difference."

I've had a couple of run-ins with those who want to argue on social media for sport. The second I realize that the conversation is taking a turn for the worse, I hop off the exit ramp and leave them to argue with themselves. Part of it is to protect my well-being, the other part is to protect my integrity and character. They'll get the hand—not the rude one in their face, but the one that waves goodbye.

Set similar boundaries around engaging with people who are unlikely to be open-minded. We all have someone in our lives where it's clear that our values are not aligned. Sometimes you may have to simply say, "Uncle John, I love you, however, I am choosing not to further this conversation because I can tell that it will not be productive. I am open to hearing you and trying to understand your perspective, but that doesn't mean that I have to agree."

Remember, when they go low EQ, you go high EQ.

Getting into heated arguments that go nowhere simply drains our energy. I'm not saying don't have discussions, but have them when you know you have the capacity for the back-and-forth. If you are aware that contention is rooted more in ignorance than hatred, provide resources and share what you have been learning in a non-judgmental way.

We all are like pebbles thrown in a pond. We can create ripple effects. You don't want to lose your witness by being antagonistic, aggressive, and abrasive. Engage with curiosity but know when to curb it when you see that the conversation is no longer productive.

BUILD COMMUNITY

There are very few things that we can do well in isolation. To keep the fire burning, it is wise to build community. Find groups that can nurture and support you. This can also include having an accountability partner who can support you in your efforts to learn and grow.

Engage in self-care activities that fuel and refresh you, and practice self-care to process unpleasant emotions that might come up for you. However, be mindful not to process your raw emotions and the weight of your awakening with those who have been systemically excluded.

They're already dealing with their trauma. They do not need to also carry the burden of your new revelations.

Use your EQ to check yourself and your motives for sharing your feelings with them. Feelings of guilt, shame, or grief can be processed with peers, family, or with a therapist. You don't want to unintentionally make it about you.

However, be careful to not use self-care as an excuse to tune out. I cannot stress this enough; addressing these institutionalized systems isn't for the faint of heart. It's much easier to bury our heads in the sand and act like everything is fine. It's not. Everything is not fine, but to mend things that are broken, we need to be well, not worn. That's why self-care is necessary.

ALLYSHIP FATIGUE

Allyship fatigue is a term that was first coined by the disability community. This term is an excuse used to justify non-participation. There's an assumption that if you read the recommended books or follow the "right people" then you are doing the work. That's not what brings about justice, equity, belonging, or safety.

As you begin doing the work of unlearning, learning, and re-learning, you might find yourself overwhelmed by your increased knowledge and awareness. At this point it seems easier to retreat back into a place of denial as a form of self-preservation. Yeah. . . Don't do that. Moral disengagement has become far too common. It's funny how quickly we move from ally to adversary whenever sacrifices need to be made.

Don't rush to the blue pill to go back into "The Matrix" when you become overwhelmed. I understand that challenging our worldview can be very emotional to process, and that the more you learn about other realities and oppressive systems, the more you will feel ill-equipped to address what seems like a formidable challenge.

Be aware of what emotions are coming up for you, assess your triggers, then address the situation in a reasonable way. Avoidance isn't the answer. Pace yourself as you gain understanding about the lived experiences of others.

Trying to dismantle systems of oppression that have been here for generations is daunting. Nevertheless, those who've been historically marginalized do not have the privilege or luxury to pivot away and disengage from their lived experiences. They will never not be exhausted. Again, don't get weary in doing what is right. We will all reap a bountiful harvest if we do not get tired of getting into good trouble.

WHY THIS MATTERS

To keep active as allies, we must also learn to care for ourselves. Staying at the front lines can cause us to grow indifferent and despondent. Having healthy self-care practices, which include community care, allows us to maintain being present and effective.

Yet we can still become inactive even with these self-care practices in place. What could possibly stand in the way of our good work?

Our good intentions.

-EQ REVIEW-

- Consistent allyship requires practicing self-care to prevent burnout.

- Burnout is the reason why 87% of peace activists quit activism within six years.

- Pacing helps to build endurance.

- Setting boundaries helps to preserve your energy. Not everyone will be open to their worldviews being challenged.

- Building community is essential to help educate and support one in their allyship journey.

- Allyship fatigue is a term that was first coined by the disability community.

- One can become overwhelmed by distressing new information about the experience of marginalized people.

- Being overwhelmed is not an excuse to cease showing up in your allyship.

- Marginalized individuals do not have the privilege to pivot from their lived experiences.

16

HOLD THE DOOR

"A good intention, with a bad approach, often leads to a poor result."

— *Thomas A. Edison*

Have you ever held the door open for someone, and they didn't say thank you? How rude, right? However, that one incident shouldn't make you slam the door in the face of the next person just because the prior person was impolite. That one encounter shouldn't change your character or your belief in common courtesy and decent behavior. At least, I hope not. So why are we so quick to call it quits when it comes to allyship work?

"I'm just not going to show up as an ally anymore," is what one White woman said to a colleague of mine. This woman had reached out to my colleague, let's call her Sandra, asking her for her opinion about an exchange she had with a Black woman online.

Sandra, who is also White, became frustrated as she realized that this stranger who direct-messaged her wasn't truly seeking perspective, but more so validation. She wanted to create an "us" versus "them" scenario, and when Sandra didn't co-sign her, the woman became upset and proceeded to resign from her performative allyship. Because that is what it was. Performative.

Performative allyship or activism is done to increase one's social capital and not because one has devoted oneself to the cause. It is to be more concerned about being perceived as being good and doing the right thing. It's often self-serving and surface-level.

If, the moment you feel you haven't been given a gold star for how you think you are showing up, and you're having misgivings about continuing in your activism, you may need to slow down and check your motives. Are your actions for show, or are they the fruit that you bear from values rooted deep within you?

Similar to Sandra's experience, a White woman sent me a private message sharing how she spent a summer marching in Black Lives Matter and Breonna Taylor protests and donated to bail funds. According to her, she also filled her social media with relevant posts and causes.

However, after months of doing this, she hadn't been able to forge any relationships with organizers or attendees. She eventually stopped trying. "I wasn't wanted in that space, probably hadn't been the whole time."

I acknowledged her feelings of rejection and asked for clarity about her decision to stop participating in social activism. She stated that she stopped participating in demonstrations, moving away from more visible support, and working more for the people immediately around her. "It's not that I don't support social justice anymore; it's more a realization that my public-facing contributions were not desired in this instance."

I reminded her that when we are addressing big issues, we believe that we need to do big gestures, like being seen. However, it's our immediate sphere of influence that can make as much or even greater impact.

No disrespect to missionaries, but there are some people of faith who feel they are doing greater work by going abroad, all while failing to care for the people within their own cities or to be a good neighbor in their own home. But I digress.

In both cases, these women highlight the fragility that arises when allyship work is driven by ego and not altruism. In allyship, there's a quieting and putting aside of your ego. I know that, in human nature, there's this question of, "What is in it for me?" This is why we must do self-checks and determine our true motives.

Are you familiar with the parable of the Good Samaritan? It tells of a traveler who is robbed, beaten, and halfway left for dead. As he lay on the road, a priest and a Levite come across the man, and they both deliberately try to avoid him, but a Samaritan sees the injured man and is moved by compassion. He treats the wounds, sets him on his donkey, takes him to an inn, and cares for him. The next day, when he leaves, he pays the host and proceeds to tell him that if there are any additional costs incurred in caring for the man, the Samaritan would pay for them as well.

In that society, the Samaritans were looked down upon. However, that didn't stop this man from using his privileges—his strength, resources, and finances—to help someone in need. His values caused him to act and be of service to someone who needed it.

GOOD INTENTIONS

There's a saying: the road to hell is paved with good intentions. If that's not the road you want to head down, then I suggest you intentionally pave a different path.

We need to recognize the difference between *intentional* and *intent*. *Intent* is a fixed thought, while *intentional* is a planned and deliberate action. Your good intention is meaningless once the action runs contrary to your intent. Intent may be your purpose; however, intentionality is done *on purpose*.

Imagine that you asked your friend Jim to help you hang some new art pieces in your living room. While hammering one of the nails, he accidentally drops the hammer, and it lands on your foot. While wincing, you tell him to be careful. Instead of an apology, his response is, "I was only trying to help." Jim's good intentions don't stop the throbbing of your baby toe. Your foot still hurts, whether he meant to harm you or not.

When someone identifies the harm you've caused, don't rush to explain how good your intent was; that matters not. An action stemming from good intent can still have a negative impact. Intentionality can decrease the probability of you doing something or saying something wrong because you are more deliberate, calculated, and conscious of the "why" behind your actions, but it does not negate harm done accidentally.

An action stemming from good intent can still have a negative impact.

Our "whys" are rooted in our values. Our values help to shape our boundaries and can drive us to act. If you value justice, inclusion, and equity, then your natural response to injustice, exclusion, and inequity will be some kind of action. The clearer we are on the things that we hold in high esteem, the more we are aware of what we will and will not accept that can keep these values from being achieved.

It's interesting how we pick and choose when and where our values are viable. I've had leaders say that they understand the importance of diversity, equity, inclusion, and belonging in the workplace, but then find it hard to apply these virtues in their personal lives because they live in communities with limited diversity.

Rarely is there a change that comes from professional development that doesn't affect your personal development. This growth and awareness should show up in all aspects of your life and naturally lend itself to other areas. If it's only showing up in one area, then is it truly authentic?

If the belief is that we can only create change in the workplace, that belief is very shortsighted. Creating psychological safety isn't confined to the professional environment. As stewards of humanity, our values guide us in creating these spaces in and out of the workplace.

What makes you care for one group of people and not the other? This requires you to audit and evaluate your values. If you truly believe everyone should be treated equally, you will not keep quiet in the face of discrimination, regardless of where you are. Choosing to only take action in a work setting or only in a certain personal setting can come off as being disingenuous and as a performative way of making you look good.

Having dialogue around DEI (diversity, equity, and inclusion) and learning within the workplace better equips you to say or do something when your family member, neighbor, or friend says something inappropriate about women, queer individuals, disabled people, and other marginalized groups.

When we focus more on being seen as good, we are less effective in our actions because we can become more centered on ourselves and less aware of how it will ultimately impact others.

For example, there was an employee who was paraplegic. At his company, they had a sliding keyboard stand that was bulky and kept hitting his knees. His company said that they would install a new one and reassured him that it would be better for him because it would be adjustable. He told his manager that he specifically preferred to put his keyboard on the desk because it allowed him to be closer to the screen. Also, he was able to better navigate his wheelchair under the desk. He requested that they remove the keyboard stand altogether so he could have more leg room.

Guess what they said? They told him, "No. This should work for you. It should be better."

Sure enough, they installed this new high-tech keyboard stand and it still ended up being unmanageable for the employee. When asked if he liked the new stand, the employee responded that it worked, but not for him. The employee ended up not using the stand at all and put the keyboard directly onto the desk as before.

This is what happens when there's a focus on doing what seems right in your own eyes without listening to others and taking into consideration how your "good deed" will impact them. If the impact is not going to serve the other person well, to hell with the good intention. It's irrelevant. If I tell you something would probably be best done one way and your response is, *I know what's better for you than you know for yourself*, then we have to chalk that up to your ego and arrogance.

Ironically, this same company, when installing automatic door openers for the restrooms, asked the same employee which side of the door should they place the button. He responded that the right-hand side would work best for him because he's right-handed; however, that doesn't mean that the next person wouldn't be left-handed. The company took note and decided to place the button on the right-hand side to accommodate their current employee. This is a reminder that we will not always get it right.

When you are in position to help and you recognize what's missing and needed for someone else's success, that's equity. In the case of a wheelchair user, being aware of accessibility in regard to ramps isn't enough. Ask the person who is going to be in need of the ramp if it's actually usable, versus having performative ramps that are unusable to any wheelchair user. And when they get off the ramp, can they easily go through the doorway? We often don't consider all the details that can impact someone until we engage with people who are living a different existence.

Part of effective communication is to actively listen, which includes asking clarifying questions. When we listen, listen to understand, so that we can gain greater insight into the needs of others.

In the example above, can we really say that his leader and others were listening to the employee? Even when he explained the issue he had with the keyboard stand, the employer heard his words but lacked understanding. I have no clue how much it cost to get this new stand, but it wasn't money well spent. Sometimes failed good intentions can be an expensive lesson.

We also do this in our personal relationships. There was a comedian who shared a story about how he bought his wife some Christian Louboutin shoes. He tried to record her reaction when she received the gift, and to his dismay, she wasn't as excited as he thought she would be. He ended up getting upset with her because he felt that she was being ungrateful. Also, because she didn't express the enthusiasm that he was expecting, he couldn't post the video on social media.

It wasn't until he put his ego aside that he was able to see the red flags, or in this case, the red bottoms, present in his situation. He admitted that his gift-giving wasn't pure. He realized that it was motivated by him wanting to show to the world that he could afford expensive shoes for his wife.

Never once did he take into consideration that the style of shoe wasn't his wife's preference, nor had she ever indicated that she desired to own a pair. Sometimes our good intentions can be pure, but we cannot ignore that there are times it's for clout. Our ability to be self-aware provides insight into why we want to do something in the first place.

We often focus on the intent behind our actions more than their effect. Because of this, we may try to excuse the outcome of our actions by using our good intentions as reasons we should not be held accountable for suboptimal outcomes.

YOU MIGHT MESS UP AND THAT'S OKAY

We don't like to feel bad about ourselves. In an effort to not feel guilt or shame, we've learned to deflect, gaslight, and make ourselves the victim. This allows us to project blame onto those we inflict pain upon to lessen the offense. This is manipulative and an act of low emotional intelligence.

Part of the discomfort we have with shame is innate, and the other part stems from our emotional narratives. For some of us, when we were growing up, we were immediately scolded and shamed when something went wrong, sometimes when it wasn't even our fault.

If we had parents and guardians who didn't practice emotional intelligence, they weren't able to teach us by effectively communicating in a way that provided the feedback, empathy, and affirmation needed to do better next time. Because mistakes weren't for learning and growth, they were avoided at all costs to bypass the emotional pain they brought.

If this is your story, I encourage you not to use it any longer as a basis to move in a spirit of offense. This lack of self-awareness and self-regulation will make it difficult for you to be corrected or teachable. You will be more risk-averse in interpersonal relationships and be conflict-avoidant. In doing so, you may end up creating more conflict and misunderstanding, which can fracture your relationships.

Learning to sit in your discomfort will help you control your emotions and improve your ability to see other perspectives. Remove excuses and commit to doing better and learning more going forward.

Guess what? There's no perfect ally. We will all fall short as we work to advocate for and elevate the voices and experiences of the underrepresented and marginalized. There will be times where you will or will not say, or do or won't do something that will negatively impact someone. Simply own up to your mistake and accept wrongdoing.

If someone acknowledges the harm you have caused by using their voice, practice the pause and check yourself. Be open to hearing and trying to understand where they are coming from.

It would be great to say that I'm a perfect wife and mother, but that isn't true. When my spouse or children tell me something I did that didn't sit well with them, I have to practice my own emotional intelligence to regulate all the feelings that come from that place of ego.

Self-justification doesn't bring about a positive outcome or change. The feedback I receive helps me figure out how I can correct my behavior so that I can continue having a harmonious relationship with them.

We learn so much by listening, being curious, and critically thinking. However, fear can make us miss opportunities to learn because it causes us to go into survival mode. When our defenses are up, we cannot see or hear clearly.

Many of us are fearful of doing or saying the wrong thing. I get that. We will inevitably make mistakes, though, and we must be willing to give ourselves grace and self-regulate our emotions of guilt or embarrassment when we do. We must let go of the desire to show up for others perfectly or look good doing so, because no one is truly good or perfect.

Learn to ask questions and say, "Please correct me if I'm saying something wrong." When you are corrected, manage your emotions so that you aren't quick to respond in a way to justify yourself. Take it. Chew on it. Digest the correction and do better the next time. If you aren't clear on what the offense was, ask if they can explain why they felt wronged.

Many like the idea of being an ally. We like the title. However, many of us don't want to do the hard work. We don't want to take the risk—and allyship is about taking risks. Showing up for others isn't easy because it requires some sort of sacrifice. In the words of Minda Harts, "No one benefits from your caution, but many benefit from your courage."

This work isn't clean. You will have to get your hands dirty. You will have to lean into your courage and discomfort and have difficult conversations with yourself and others. You may have to do difficult things.

I hope we can agree that working toward creating a better world that is anti-racist, anti-sexist, anti-homophobic, anti-ableist, means that we all need to be open to being teachable, understanding that there will be times we will need to be corrected and not take offense. Of course, when correcting others, do so with grace. Yes, there's so much to be righteously angry about, but there's room for us to use our emotional intelligence and be gracious in the way we correct others.

WHY IT MATTERS

Allyship rooted in our ego will cause us to be ineffective, inconsistent, and disingenuous. Assessing our values and using our emotional intelligence will help us remain steadfast, agile, and open to correction.

The better we understand that allyship requires patience, persistence, and grace to and for one another, it will allow us to be more teachable and to genuinely support each other.

EQ-Tip

Three ways you can put your allyship into action:

INDIVIDUALLY - Use inclusive language. For example, in lieu of mankind, use humankind; husband/wife - partner; maiden name - family name

Challenge your bias, educate yourself, learn about your privilege, study historical challenges of marginalized people, learn from your mistakes, diversify your work, and don't assume gender.

Learning about other peoples' experiences increases empathy and understanding.

Representation in imagery.

INTERPERSONALLY – Examples are: correcting a colleague who assumes someone's gender, mentoring a colleague and making sure they get credit for their contributions, and affirming someone's experience of inequity.

Remember, no two people or situations are alike. It's always important to think of the individual you are supporting. Ask yourself, what barriers are they facing? What's your relationship with them?

STRUCTURALLY – Examples are: advocating for objective hiring and promotions, accessible technology and tools for people with disabilities, learning what solutions historically marginalized people are working on, and learning to align your work with theirs.

-EQ REVIEW-

- There's a difference between intentional and intent.

- Intent may be your purpose, however, intentionality is done *on* purpose.

- Assess your motives behind your allyship work.

- Performative allyship or activism is done to increase one's social capital and not because one has devoted themselves to the cause.

- Allyship requires you to listen to those who you are trying to serve.

- Allyship isn't about perfection, it's about persistence. Prepare to mess up.

- Allyship requires sacrifice.

17

NOBODY IS STANDING HERE

"I always wondered 'why somebody didn't do something about that.'
Then I realized I was somebody."

— Lily Tomlin

Well, my friend, this is where we part. I thank you for letting me walk with you (and your dog) as we traveled down this emotional intelligence road.

I'm proud of you for pressing forward and being courageous in stepping out of your comfort zone.

It's not always easy to acknowledge our feelings. We learned in Part One that our feelings didn't just show up today. Our connection to and disconnection from them comes from our past.

Our emotional narratives play a significant role in how we exercise our emotional intelligence, and we cannot ignore the impact of our upbringing and our culture when putting this skill set into practice.

There are many barriers to equity that need to be broken down. Our emotional intelligence can be one of our greatest tools in addressing inequities.

We now understand that, just like we don't season our chicken in the same way, due to inequity, there are those of us who use emotional intelligence differently.

For far too long, this skill has been used for survival by those who have been purposely pushed to the margins. It has been used to survive enslavement, genocide, and violence and to strategically navigate through minefields of microaggressions.

It is time to begin using your emotional intelligence for your healing and well-being.

For far too long, groups of people have been quieted and excluded because others didn't want them to take up space. . . not realizing that there's plenty of room.

For far too long, we've been comfortable with the mainstream ideologies, leaving our biases unchecked because we didn't want the discomfort of elevating our awareness so that we would have to address reality. Now that you've come to this point where you are thinking differently and feeling differently, it's up to you to *do* differently.

I've talked about literal and figurative rooms, but, now, I'm talking about the global room that we call our world. I know that they are planning future flights to Mars, but, for right now, there's no other planet you can go to and live on. Earth is it!

Our collective low emotional intelligence has led to genocide, allowed disease to spread, children to suffer, increased mental health crises,, triggered natural disasters, and caused wildlife to become extinct. We have failed to show up for one another, which, in essence, means we have also failed to show up for ourselves.

If we really want to see a different future where our true values are lived out and aren't just lip service, then we all need to elevate our emotional intelligence. I hope that you recognize that this skill goes far beyond being a high performer in the workplace. It's about performing great acts of kindness and empathy that impact not only you but your family, friends, and everyone around you.

I think back to Minda Harts' revelation regarding others not being able to show up for her when she was racially discriminated against in the workplace because they possibly had low emotional intelligence themselves. They didn't know how to regulate their emotions; therefore, although it pained them to witness the discrimination against her, they didn't have the tools to address it and act.

Maybe you can relate. Maybe you've been one of those people who remained silent in the presence of injustice and bad actors. We all have moments when we wish we had done something differently. I'm not here to dredge up regret. I'm lovingly placing my hand on your shoulder to call out that feeling of shame and replace it with conviction.

We're trying to change and disrupt the systems that continuously oppress and frustrate the advancement of people. Because of these discriminatory systems, many who've been marginalized and othered falsely believe that they are imposters and that they don't belong, because that's what the people in the room keep telling them.

If we have more people in the room saying, "You belong here. We are intentionally working on creating a space where you are safe to show up as your best self," that's how we move into real change. To create belonging, you need to address the people doing the excluding.

Allyship isn't restricted to White men and women; it's all our responsibility. The power of privilege ascends beyond race. You may not be White, male, non-disabled, neurotypical, or heterosexual, but you still have agency, privilege, and can make an impact. We aren't allying to advance one cause or one race; we are allies for the human race.

However, we must recognize that the current systems benefit heterosexual, cisgender, White males, putting them in a position to make the most impact as allies. When these men go to work, an email, a phone call, or a meeting changes everything. It isn't fair, but that doesn't make it less true.

Remember the White gentleman who used his privilege to advocate for the promotion of a Black woman whose workplace was denying her advancement? He did so not because he wanted to be perceived as an ally or a "good White person." It was because he believed it was the right thing to do. He served from an authentic place. When you see something wrong that you wouldn't accept for yourself, then, ask yourself, "Well, why would I accept it for someone else?"

During one of my professional trainings, I share a clip from an interview with Amandla Stenberg and Trevor Noah on *The Daily Show*. Amandla plays the lead in the movie *The Hate You Give*, based on Angie Thomas' first novel by the same title. It's a story about a sixteen-year-old girl who grapples with racism, identity, police brutality, and activism after witnessing the police murder her childhood friend.

In one of the final questions of the interview, Noah asks Stenberg, "What would you say your greatest hope and success would have been besides White people crying?"

Stenberg and the studio audience chuckle.

Trevor smiles and continues, "When people watch *The Hate You Give*, what do you want them to walk away with?"

Amandla replies, "Well, I mean, White people crying actually was the goal."

Both Trevor and the audience erupt with laughter. Every time, my attendees laugh along with them. After the clip, I ask, "Why does it take a movie to garner empathy for Black life?"

Yeah, that sucks the air out of the room quickly.

The tears may be genuine, but, just because you are moved, that doesn't always mean it caused you to move and take intentional action.

In the wake of the racial unrest of 2020, many organizations held "listening sessions" and "healing circles." As a clinician and workplace well-being consultant, I was asked to lead several of these. Don't get me wrong, some of these were beneficial; however, as time went on, these workplace events became more a form of trauma porn than any real catalyst for change.

For what seemed like the first time, the experience of Black people was in the spotlight. However, it was an exhibition of pain. Onlookers were able to maintain their distance as they watched and listened from the comfort of their homes while Black colleagues shared their suffering via Zoom.

Unfortunately, it didn't take long before resentment emerged. Employees began to grumble. "Why is it always about Black people? What about (insert another marginalized group)?"

You may be wondering the same thing too. If so, I encourage you to slow your amygdala down. Breathe and ask yourself this question: "Within each marginalized group, who is the *most* marginalized and underrepresented?"

Taking a moment to think critically and read the room, you will realize that regardless of race, gender, sexuality, disability, or other intersectional characteristics, the least of these will be a Black person—more than likely, a Black woman. Meaning, if we approach the systemic issues that impact Black people with emotional intelligence, we can address the issues that impact many others.

However, I've recognized that, unless you give examples to which people can relate, it can be challenging for others to empathize with another person's perspective and experience. I'm acutely aware that when the subject of racism comes up, the default is for some to become defensive.

When highlighting the Black experience, it becomes evident that some want to play "marginalized metrics"—a fruitless game of comparing oppression that leaves little room for empathy by building a hierarchy of pain. So, we come up with examples, hoping that in one of them, you can see yourself because, sadly, we default to being self-centered.

So, which one are you? The short person who needs help reaching for something on the top shelf? Maybe you're the left-handed person, frustrated by how the rings on the left side of the notebook remind you that its intended user isn't you. Perhaps you're the one who's hard of hearing and is burdened with the task of asking for closed captions to be turned on or that someone keep their webcam on so that you can read their lips.

As I've said before, things don't become dear to us unless they become near to us. As we discussed in Part One of this book, there are several barriers to having emotional intelligence, and unfortunately, as good as we may think we are, we often can't see past our own noses. Not only that, if we've been taught that certain people who are different from us are less than us, then it will be increasingly difficult to empathize.

There are social narratives that reaffirm this belief, that range from sharing postcards of Black people being lynched to the racial bias in the medical field, where Black bodies are experimented on and believed to experience less pain.

I know that you may want to refute the notion that you could possibly, in some secret part of you, believe that a Black or other racialized person is not your equal. That they don't have the same human value as you do. But what if? What if that could be it? We've seen more people move to action in the name of animal cruelty than we have for our fellow man.

There's a video of American diversity educator Jane Elliot, where she asks White audience members to stand if they would be happy receiving the same treatment that Black citizens do in this society. No one stands.

She repeats the question, and still, no one moves.

She exclaims, "Nobody's standing here."

She then states, "That says very plainly that you know what's happening."

After a brief pause, she continues, "You know you don't want it for you. I want to know why you're so willing to accept it. . . for others."

Why are we willing to accept it and allow it for others?

We cannot be good stewards and create a world that is psychologically safe without being emotionally intelligent. This skill requires us to truly look within while simultaneously analyzing the data we receive from others.

It makes us check our hypocrisy. We cannot live in cognitive dissonance when we are self-aware. When we are given the right feedback and our efforts are reinforced, we're able to become more resilient and courageous in how we show up for ourselves and others.

Emotional intelligence can be a driver to act, helping us become more aware of how our values align with our actions. It only really works when everyone is practicing it, not just one person.

I am reminded of Martin Neimöller's famous post-war words:

First they came for the socialists, and I did not speak out –
because I was not a socialist.
Then they came for the trade unionists, and I did not speak out –
because I was not a trade unionist.
Then they came for the Jews, and I did not speak out –
because I was not a Jew.
Then they came for me—and there was no one left to speak for me.

How can we truly treat each other humanely if we do not see others as fully human?

Our emotional intelligence has suffered from a sad case of glaucoma and color blindness that has deteriorated our ability to see each other clearly. When flashes of reality come into our sight, we request blindness once more, hoping to unsee the role we play that silences, disenfranchises, marginalizes, discriminates against, and ignores certain humans.

Elevating our awareness can be uncomfortable, but it is necessary. You can choose to put on rose-colored glasses and pop the blue pill to return to the *Matrix* of complacency if you'd like. Yet, if you've come to this point of the book, you would have to ask yourself, "Why?"

Why do I want to return to ignorance? Do I value convenience and comfort more than justice and righteousness? If I feel this way, how many more are choosing their comfort over the well-being of others? What would happen then? What would our world look like?

I can answer that. Look around.

DEAR READER/
A NOTE FROM THE AUTHOR

This book took longer than expected.

I suspect many authors say this.

What I thought would take six months, with discipline and faithfulness, took almost two years.

It didn't matter how badly I wanted to finish the book. There were moments when I just had no more "go" in me. I had to honor that and stop.

I couldn't write a book on emotional intelligence and not practice it.

Several times, I had to practice the pause and ask, "How am I feeling?"; "What do I need right now?"; "Am I out of alignment?"

I experienced burnout—maternal burnout and from book writing.

I wrestled with depression—seasonal depression and the one that likes to swing by without calling first.

I wanted to quit—I really convinced myself that y'all *really* didn't need this book.

Although I gave myself grace, these fits and starts were frustrating. Managing my roles as a mother, wife, and CEO in a whole hot panini of a pandemic, I was curious as to why writing seemed "so hard!"

It was in the conversations I had with my dear friend, Sarah Noll Wilson, where she wondered if it was possible that I was neurodivergent.

She had shared with me how she came to get her late diagnosis of ADHD. There were numerous occasions during our discussions when I thought, *Well, that sounds familiar.*

I had already planned to get our eldest evaluated for ADHD due to what I had observed while homeschooling, so I scheduled an evaluation for myself.

It turns out I do have ADHD. (Honestly, I'm not surprised).

This diagnosis provided an additional layer of awareness as to why I do the things I do, but now I see how it impacts my mood and productivity.

I love the waves of hyper-focus, but I must be mindful that if I don't practice the pause and intentionally take breaks, there will be an unfortunate crash or withdrawal after the high.

I began to understand that my interest-seeking brain would sometimes get bored by the book-writing process and try to chase other rabbits.

I learned that if I felt like the challenge was "too hard," I couldn't force myself to do it.

I've shared with my book launch partners that I didn't want to give them a book that was crispy and smoky because it was birthed from burnout. My EQ taught me to take the long route and trust that I would get to the destination at the appointed time.

The time is now.

I also wrestled with the tone in which to write this book.

When writing about marginalized people, do I use "they" and "them" or "we" and "us?" Trust me, it makes a difference.

My concern is that, when writing, for example, about the Black experience or that of women, using the third person distanced me from the group.

I had to reflect on whether writing in this manner centered the "majority" and prioritized their comfort.

This was my attempt to read the room as I welcomed you into this space as the reader. I'm still pondering on this now.

Let's look at these sentences from Chapter 9, for example:

> *"Those from racially marginalized groups have learned at a young age that their feelings are less valid than their White counterparts. They witness how their White classmates are extended grace while they are subjected to harsher discipline."*

What if I had written it this way:

> *"For those of us who've been racially marginalized, we've learned at a young age that our feelings are less valid than our White counterparts. We've witnessed how our White classmates are extended grace while we're subjected to harsher discipline."*

How did reading this second example land on you? Practice the three A's. Can you name the feeling and why you're experiencing that particular emotion?

Did your emotional reaction intensify? Was that dog tugging at you?

Depending on who you are, these words made you feel more connected to or disconnected from me as the author.

It was these sentences that made me stop in my tracks.

As I began rewriting my entire book, I was repositioning myself not only as the author but also as the subject about whom I was writing.

I asked myself whether I wanted to challenge the reader to read with this new tone. Would I overly trigger their amygdala? Would this help to elevate the voices of those who have been pushed to the margins and center their voices, our voices, even more?

I don't have any answers for you.

I can't tell you whether there is a right or wrong approach. I simply wanted to share my process with you. I wanted to share how I practiced my own EQ when I was considering you.

I am still learning. I hope my book inspired you to learn more, too.

BIBLIOGRAPHY

Braveman, P. A., Arkin, E., Proctor, D., Kauh, T., & Holm, N. (2022). Systemic And Structural Racism: Definitions, Examples, Health Damages, And Approaches To Dismantling. *Health Affairs*, *41*(2), 171–178. https://www.healthaffairs.org/doi/10.1377/hlthaff.2021.01394

Dawson, G. A., Karl, K. A., & Peluchette, J. V. (2019). Hair Matters: Toward Understanding Natural Black Hair Bias in the Workplace. *Journal of Leadership & Organizational Studies*, *26*(3), 389–401. https://journals.sagepub.com/doi/10.1177/1548051819848998

Harmon, A., & Burch, A. D. S. (2020, June 22). White Americans Say They Are Waking Up to Racism. What Will It Add Up To? *The New York Times*. https://www.nytimes.com/2020/06/22/us/racism-white-americans.html

McCluney, C. L., Durkee, M. I., Smith, R. E., Robotham, K. J., & Lee, S. S.-L. (2021). To be, or not to be…Black: The effects of racial codeswitching on perceived professionalism in the workplace. *Journal of Experimental Social Psychology*, *97*(97), 104199 https://www.sciencedirect.com/science/article/abs/pii/S002210312 1001025?via%3Dihub

Mental Health America. (2022). *Racial Trauma*. Mental Health America. https://www.mhanational.org/racial-trauma

President, M. J. C., CEO &. (2019, July 1). *Unconscious Bias | Employee Workshops | DEI Consultants*. The Percipio Company. https://percipiocompany.com/if-you-have-a-brain-you-have-bias/#:~:text=Our%20brains%20navigate%2011%2C000%2C000%20bits, cognitive%20biases%20are%20the%20result

Preventing Burnout. (n.d.). Effective Activist. https://effectiveactivist.com/movements/burnout/#:~:text=Unfortunately%2C%20burnout%20is%20quite%20common,6%20years%20of%20getting%20involved

Racial differences in weathering and its associations with psychosocial stress: The CARDIA study. (2019). *SSM - Population Health*, *7*, 100319. https://www.sciencedirect.com/science/article/pii/S2352827318302246

Sarafim-Silva, B. A. M., & Bernabé, D. G. (2021). Emotional Intelligence for Coping with the Consequences of Childhood Trauma. In *www.intechopen.com*. IntechOpen. https://www.intechopen.com/chapters/76847

Shensa, A., Sidani, J. E., Dew, M. A., Escobar-Viera, C. G., & Primack, B. A. (2018). Social Media Use and Depression and Anxiety Symptoms: A Cluster Analysis. *American Journal of Health Behavior*, *42*(2), 116–128. https://www.ncbi.nlm.nih.gov/pmc/articles/PMC5904786/

"Weathering": The health effects of stress and discrimination. (2021, February 26). Www.medicalnewstoday.com. https://www.medicalnewstoday.com/articles/weathering-what-are-the-health-effects-of-stress-and-discrimination

ACKNOWLEDGMENTS

It is a blessing to know that you are loved and cared for without a shadow of a doubt.

I don't take it lightly, as I know that there are many who wonder if they are truly loved and if they matter to someone.

I believe in giving people their flowers while they can still smell them. So here we go.

Oh! If by chance I forgot to mention you, charge my head, not my heart.

To My Interviewees:

Thank you for sharing your time, expertise, and experiences with me. You helped my book come alive with your stories, truth, and knowledge. I'm grateful that you said yes to being a part of this project.

To My Review Board:

Thank you Sacha Thompson, Lionel Allen, and Natasha Miller Williams, for helping me get the best version of the book out of me. Your thoughts, edits, and feedback were all necessary to make each revision better.

Special shout out to my writing coach Cathy Fyock. You had the patience of Job but never stopped encouraging me to keep going. You gave me the space that I needed and provided a community of authors who helped to remind me that I wasn't alone.

To My Day Ones:

It doesn't matter how long it's been since the last time we spoke, or how far the distance: when we connect, it's as if no time has passed. Decades have passed, and the music of life may change, but we never skip a beat.

Erlene Cox, thank you for ALWAYS making me laugh! We've gone through so many seasons together, and will go through so many more. We have rejoiced and mourned together over these past thirty plus years. I love you til' the world blow up!

Sheena McClain, thank you for always cheering me on and believing in me. I love you so much.

James Jolly, my brother from another mother. Thank you for trusting that I could do this crazy thing. I love that our love for each other has kept this friendship going despite the distance.

To My PUSH (Pray Until Something Happens) Partners/ Midwives:

Whenever you are trying to birth something, you need support. The labor pains were uncomfortable, yet, I had these beautiful women right there with me.

In no particular order, I want to thank you:

Elizabeth Goueti, my sister from another mister. You're a gift that keeps giving. I'm so glad that in 2017 we decided to invest in a friendship after that Lisa Nichols conference. Thank you for putting "Best Selling Author" as my contact name in your phone, LOL.

Veronica Jenkins, it's amazing how one can build a connection with someone they've never met. I pray that, by the time this book is released, we will have seen each other face to face.

Vladimire Calixte, you covered me in ways that blew my mind. I praise God for you and His hand over your life. Thank you for speaking life into me.

Marline François-Madden, thank you for all of your encouragement.

Patricia Cerenil, thank you for being your beautiful, genuine self. Thank you for your prayers.

To Tati Dieula and Nennen Cici, thank you for checking in and praying for me during this process. I cherish your special love for me.

Sharlisa Grant, GIRL! Please know that I see you, I love you so much, and greatness is in you! I have been blessed by your continued encouragement and belief in me. Your words and prayers are so precious to me.

Kelley Bonner, thank you for the encouragement and insights you brought to this book.

Erica Reed, your prayers, big sister love, and encouragement, I truly treasure.

And to Keshia Harris, my beautiful sister-in-love, whew! You inspire me so much. You always had an on-time word of encouragement that soothed my soul. How I love you!

To My Sara(h)s:

I don't think I would have made it this far without you.

Sara Elysée, from the beginning of this project and all the way through, you were the only one that I didn't mind asking me, "How's the book coming along?" I dreaded this question from most, but I welcomed it from you because I knew your inquiry came from such a gentle, tender, and pure place. There weren't any expectations attached, just a loving nudge to push me further. You were so excited about this book that I felt that I had to finish it just so I wouldn't disappoint you.

Sarah Noll Wilson, I found you suddenly, but it feels like you've always been here. I thank you for your generosity of heart, experience, and time. You've rooted for me every step of the way, sat with me as I processed deeply how best to articulate a thing, and assured me that I was on the right track. There's so much muchness in our friendship yet, words fail me. Please know that this project wouldn't be where it is without you.

Sarah Strezo, my amazing photographer! Lady, you got me looking good! The fact that you were more excited about our shoots than I was just tickles me. Thank you for making time in front of the camera so fun. Not only that, once you found out I was writing a book, you have been so supportive. I am excited about where our new found relationship will go!

To My Families:

Mom and Dad, thank you for all the sacrifices you made so that your children can have the life you dreamed of. When you left Haiti, you had no clue what the future held, but you believed for the better. Thank you for providing us with a nurturing home filled with constant affirmation, love, and respect toward us children. Although I know that you are proud of me for this accomplishment, thank you that your love for your children was never based on what we did but because of who we are – your children. Your belief in me has anchored me in more ways than you know. I know who I am because of you.

Ness, you are the best taller little sister, turned copyeditor, web designer, project manager, sounding board, and everything in between. Thank you.

To Ruby, thank you for your resolute and positive mindset and quiet love that can be felt in every hug. Thank you for believing in me.

And to my Harris family. Thank you for welcoming me in and loving and supporting me like I was one of your own.

To My Littles:

Mommy loves you and mommy thanks you. You blessed me every time you'd peek into my room and say, "Hope you're doing good with your work." The writing process was slower because sometimes I had to just stop so I could mother, and I'm sorry that there were times I didn't stop more. Thank you for your grace. I hope and pray that birthing this book will bear good fruit that will bless your lives in ways I cannot even imagine.

To My Michael:

What do I say to you? We've already had a trove of words we have shared between us. But, let's be honest, this hasn't been easy. As much as our children gave me grace, you extended more. Thank you for praying for me. For your unwavering faith in me. I can do hard things because of you. Thank you for being my person. Thank you for the fact that, even when it seemed that this project took me away more than any of us wanted, you never told me to stop. You continue to prove that choosing to do life with you was and will always be my best decision. It is an honor to love and be loved by you. I love you VML. #TeamHarris.

APPENDIX A: EQ EXERCISES

Exercise #1

Choose five to seven individuals (feel free to choose more) from various areas of your life. For example, family, colleagues, friends, mentors, mentees, and team members. Ask for feedback on how they perceive you.

You can ask them these questions directly, or if you're feeling fancy, create a survey and have them fill it out anonymously.

The goal is to assess how different your perception of yourself is from others' perceptions of you.

Some questions you could ask:

1. What three words would you use to describe me?
2. What was your first impression of me?
3. What do I do well?
4. What areas do you think I could improve on?
5. When you're around me, how do I make you feel?
6. What's something I do that frustrates or annoys you?
7. Would you describe me as passive, passive-aggressive, aggressive, or assertive?

After you do this exercise, you can't get stuck in awareness. Remember the three A's? You can implement them here as well.

<u>Awareness:</u> Collection of responses.

<u>Assessment:</u> Summarize the takeaways. What do they mean? Were there things that surprised you? Is there alignment between how you view yourself and how others view you?

<u>Action:</u> You can't stay at awareness. In terms of behavior change, how can you reinforce your strengths and shore up your weaknesses? This is where we put action into motion. What are your next steps?

For example, perhaps you speak over others. You can work on being more patient in conversations by pausing and counting to five before speaking.

Exercise #2

Being able to manage and regulate our emotions takes practice. Consider a few grounding exercises if humming doesn't come naturally to you.

- Practice the pause and name five things you can see, feel, smell, and hear around the room.
- Take five to ten deep cleansing breaths. You can do this by breathing in through your nose for 5 seconds while filling your diaphragm. Hold that breath for 5 seconds, and then exhale through your mouth for 5 seconds.
- Listen to relaxing music.
- Go for a walk or run.
- Write out your feelings.

Let's have a moment of reflection. Can you identify your default emotion? This is the feeling that you often go to when you are stressed. For example, if it is anger:

- Think of a time when you were angry and how you handled it.
- Think about how you would like to process anger in the future.
- Identify what your emotional triggers are. (ex: Feeling invisible, being controlled, being dismissed)
  o Additional triggers can be familiar sounds, scents, or sights.

Exercise #3

Here are some activities you can do to improve your relationship management skills.

- Review activities on self-awareness.
- Review activities on feedback.
- Review social awareness activities to help you pay more attention to others' feelings.
- Practice actively listening. If you are a person that finds yourself often interrupting others, slow yourself down and count to five in your head to make sure that the other person has finished their thought.
- Ask clarifying questions. Ex: "What I hear you saying is _____. Is that correct?"
- Minimize distractions when speaking with others. Turn off the television, put your phone down or on "Do Not Disturb," and if possible, turn your body to face them to show that you are giving them your full attention.
- Set clear expectations. No one is a mind reader. Articulate what it is that you are expecting in a role, task, or behavior. Clarifying these responsibilities minimizes confusion and disappointment.
- Identify someone's love language. Our "love language" describes how we receive love from others, but it isn't only for romantic relationships. Knowing if words of affirmation, gift-giving, quality time, physical touch, or acts of service are what motivates or fills someone's cup can help improve your relationship with them.

Exercise #4

If you've never thought about how your past impacts your current responses to people and situations, I urge you to do so. Take a moment to write or dictate your emotional narrative.

Some questions to ask yourself:

1. What did I learn about feelings from my. . .
   a. Family?
   b. Friends?
   c. School?
   d. Society?
2. What emotions were accepted?
3. What emotions weren't accepted?
4. How did the adults in my life express their feelings? Passive aggressively? Violently?
5. How were they discussed? Was it in an open and direct manner?
6. How were emotions used?
7. What didn't I learn about feelings?
8. How comfortable am I expressing my emotions?
9. How comfortable am I experiencing the emotions of others?

APPENDIX B: THERAPY DIRECTORIES

Inclusivetherapists.com

Latinxtherapy.com

Therapyforblackgirls.com

Cliniciansofcolor.org

Melaninandmentalhealth.com

Therapyforblackmen.org

asianmhc.org/apisaa

Beam.community

Nqttcn.com

Lgbtqpscyhotherapitsofcolor.com

muslimmentalhealth.com

Nativepsychs.org

Muslimmentalhealth.com

Ayanatherapy.com

Psychologytoday.com

Review Inquiry

Hey, it's Farah here.

I hope you've enjoyed the book, finding it both useful and challenging. I have a favor to ask you.

Would you consider giving it a rating wherever you bought the book? Online book stores are more likely to promote a book when they feel good about its content, and reader reviews are a great barometer for a book's quality.

So please go to the website of wherever you bought the book, search for my name and the book title, and leave a review. If able, perhaps consider adding a picture of you holding the book. That increases the likelihood your review will be accepted!

Many thanks in advance,

Farah Harris

Will You Share the Love?

Get this book for a friend, associate, or family member!

If you have found this book valuable and know others who would find it useful, consider buying them a copy as a gift. Special bulk discounts are available if you would like your whole team or organization to benefit from reading this. Just contact info@workingwelldaily.com or visit workingwelldaily.com.

Would You Like Farah Harris to Speak to Your Organization?

Book Farah Now!

Farah accepts a limited number of speaking and training engagements each year. To learn how you can bring her message to your organization, email info@workingwelldaily.com or visit workingwelldaily.com.

ABOUT THE AUTHOR

Farah Harris, MA, LCPC, is a Belonging and Workplace Well-being expert and a licensed psychotherapist with over 12 years of experience. She has certifications in neuroscience, psychological safety, and diversity, equity, and inclusion. She works with DEI practitioners and leaders of Fortune 500 companies who recognize that the work landscape has changed and that wellness perks don't fix wellness problems. These companies want to sustain a healthy and inclusive work environment where employees and applicants know it isn't lip service or an initiative and that belonging and balance are valued.

As a clinician, Farah is acutely aware of how the workplace impacts the health of individuals and how it spills over to their performance, productivity, and overall job satisfaction when they do not feel seen, heard, or respected. She addresses this through educational lectures, keynotes, training, coaching, and consulting, cultivating curious and courageous conversations and enhancing professional development and personal growth.

Farah is a contributing writer for Fast Company. Her work has been featured in media and podcasts such as Forbes, Business Insider, Harvard Business Review, Good Morning America, Essence, Huffington

Post, Thrive Global, Therapy for Black Girls, and American Negotiation Institute.

Farah holds a bachelor's degree in Economics pre-Law, one in Marketing Management, and a master's degree in Mental Health Counseling.

She was born in Haiti and raised in the north shore suburbs of Chicago. Farah now resides in the Chicagoland area with her husband and three children.

Farah can be reached at: workingwelldaily.com